WITNESS TO THE MARTYRDOM

John Taylor

WITNESS TO THE MARTYRDOM

JOHN TAYLOR'S PERSONAL ACCOUNT OF THE LAST DAYS
OF THE PROPHET JOSEPH SMITH

———

BY ELDER JOHN TAYLOR
OF THE COUNCIL OF THE TWELVE APOSTLES

Compiled and edited by Mark H. Taylor

Deseret Book Company • Salt Lake City, Utah

Library of Congress Cataloging-in-Publication Data

Taylor, John, 1808–1887.

    Witness to the martyrdom : John Taylor's personal account of the last days of the prophet Joseph Smith / edited and compiled by Mark H. Taylor.

      p.   cm.

    Includes bibliographical references and index.

    ISBN 1-57345-449-4

    1. Taylor, John, 1808–1887. 2. Smith, Joseph, 1805–1844—Assassination. 3. Mormons—Illinois—Carthage—Biography. 4. Mormon Church—Presidents—Biography. I. Taylor, Mark H. 1964–   . II. Title.

BX8695.T3A3   1999

289.3'092—dc21

[B]   98-56103
                                                    CIP

Printed in the United States of America   49510-6428

10 9 8 7 6 5 4 3 2

To Rozann, Sterling, Candace,
Preston, and Braden

CONTENTS

CONTENTS

PREFACE

My interest in the story of the martyrdom of Joseph Smith as told by John Taylor (hereafter referred to as the Martyrdom Manuscript) began when I read *The Life of John Taylor* as a young boy. My parents presented me with my own copy of the biography of my great-great-grandfather, and I read the book through. Upon reading of Elder Taylor's experiences in Carthage as he was brought to the junction of mortality and eternity, I gained a new sense of my ancestral roots and a deeper appreciation of the gospel. The emotions that accompanied my reading of the events surrounding the Martyrdom cemented their significance in my young mind. My parents taught me that as a recipient of the blessings of the gospel, I had a significant responsibility to honor and remember all that my ancestors and countless other pioneers had freely given, including their lives in many cases, to the building up of the Church. I haven't always been successful at fulfilling that responsibility, but in the attempt, the fires of testimony ignited within my heart as a youth and have continued to brighten ever since.

PREFACE

A copy of an abbreviated version of the Martyrdom Manuscript had circulated in our family circles for decades. It became significant to me after reading some of the excerpts of the text which had been included in *The Life of John Taylor.* I read it frequently in my youth and filed a copy of it with my other family history materials. However, I did not encounter the complete manuscript until recently. By then, I had consistently been carrying copies of that abbreviated version for several years to share with potential missionary contacts and others who might be interested in the account. In 1996 and 1997 I renewed my interest in sharing that version with nonmembers and members alike, as enthusiasm for the activities associated with the pioneer sesquicentennial celebrations escalated in Iowa and Nebraska. With that renewal of interest, I determined that I should attempt to find the complete version. I retrieved the original copy of the abbreviated version that I had retained from my youth; on it I found a note at the bottom that led me to a book published in 1862 that contained the completed version. When I located a copy of that book and read the account, I was deeply moved. It did not take long to determine that the time to help share the significance of that treasure on a broader scale was long overdue.

My interest in the Manuscript is not in harboring ill feelings toward Joseph's enemies from those difficult days. Rather, it is in the preserving the witness that the Manuscript provides of an "overruling Providence" in the events that occurred; it is in its witness of the noble and honorable way in which the brethren conducted themselves during their darkest hours; it is in preserving the memory

and the legacy of Joseph Smith. The Martyrdom
Manuscript attests to a great legacy that has been left to us
as beneficiaries of the promised latter-day restoration.
Through it, we can realize something of the terrible costs of
the Restoration and build our faith in its authenticity. It is
my hope that those who read and experience the
Martyrdom Manuscript might more fully understand and
appreciate the depth and breadth of the legacy that has
been left for us as members of The Church of Jesus Christ
of Latter-day Saints.

In preparing this work, I received the help and advice of
many individuals, without which this book would not have
been completed. My parents, Robert E. Taylor and Margaret
M. Hedin Taylor, provided an important foundation for my
involvement with this manuscript.

My wife, Rozann, and our children, Sterling, Candace,
Preston, and Braden, have taught me a great deal about
charity and love and faith. Through them I have learned
what matters most in life. During the process of completing
this work, as with all of the aspects of my life, they provided
special encouragement.

Part 1

EDITOR'S INTRODUCTION

O n 27 June 1844, at approximately 5:16 P.M., Joseph Smith, Jr., the prophet, seer, and revelator of the dispensation of the fulness of times and founder of The Church of Jesus Christ of Latter-day Saints, and Hyrum Smith, Joseph's brother and the patriarch of the Church, were brutally murdered in the jail in Carthage, Illinois, by an armed mob. This event is irrevocably singular in the destinies of The Church of Jesus Christ of Latter-day Saints. By it Joseph Smith sealed his testimony of the great latter-day restoration of the gospel of Jesus Christ with his own blood. Through it the early Saints experienced the refiner's fire, which helped them prepare for the trials of the coming westward migration to the safety of the Rocky Mountains.

Joseph's persecutors conceived that his demise would be the Church's demise, immediately putting an end to the "Mormon question." Few Church members in Joseph's day, not to mention his persecutors, would have predicted that in just over 150 years subsequent to his death, the latter-day stone—cut out of the mountain without hands—would roll forth to consume the earth and that the Church would "come forth out of the wilderness of darkness, and shine forth fair as the moon, clear as the sun."[1]

Clearly Joseph's principal persecutors could not have anticipated the esteem with which he is now held in the minds of millions across the earth, both in and out of the Church. Indeed, Joseph's name today is "had for good and evil among all nations."[2]

At the time of the Martyrdom, most of the leaders of the Church were away from the vicinity of Nauvoo. The majority of the Twelve were on missions to the East. Because of their unique assignments, however, two of the Twelve had remained behind: Willard Richards, secretary to Joseph Smith, and John Taylor, editor and publisher of the *Times and Seasons* and the *Nauvoo Neighbour*. In the midst of the difficult circumstances, the brethren determined to go to Carthage to place themselves under the immediate protection of Illinois Governor Thomas Ford, in hopes that somehow the difficulties might be peacefully resolved. At Joseph's request, Elders Richards and Taylor accompanied him to Carthage to meet with the governor and to witness the sufferings and trauma of what they hoped would never occur but perhaps somewhat anticipated.

In addition to the two apostles, several other brethren visited Joseph and Hyrum in the jail during the few days prior to the Martyrdom. However, only Willard Richards and John Taylor were with the Smiths when the assault occurred, since the other brethren had departed on errands and the mob forbade their return.

The mob had strategically isolated the four brethren that constituted the leadership of the Church remaining in Nauvoo. Their intent was to leave *no* survivors; however, the heavens had other plans. Willard Richards escaped virtually unscathed, but the mob's bullets found their mark on the person of Elder John Taylor five times, four of which caused terrible injury. So severe were his wounds that he nearly lost his life. Notwithstanding, by "a special act of mercy," Providence preserved him. Somewhat physically disabled by the effects of his wounds, Elder Taylor became a living martyr, esteemed as a special witness to the events of Carthage for the remainder of his life. The timepiece he carried in his breast pocket during the massacre and which was hit by one of the mob's bullets is, at the time of this writing, prominently displayed in the Church Historical Museum in Salt Lake City, Utah. It has been the object of reverent curiosity for hundreds of thousands, perhaps millions, of members of the Church.

Despite having a basic understanding of the pivotal events that occurred at Carthage and their relationship to the development, movement, and destinies of the Church, most members of the Church do not have a complete knowledge of the events that led to and climaxed in the martyrdom. The answers to questions such as why the brethren abandoned the safety of Nauvoo and went to Carthage in the first place, or why they were incarcerated, etc., have remained somewhat obscure. Without a clear understanding of all the factors involved, it is difficult to comprehend how the numerous conditions and factors embedded in those events culminated in the Prophet's death.

Misunderstanding is also evident regarding the full extent of the miraculous role that Elder Taylor's timepiece played in the preservation of his life, and the extreme extent of his wounds and suffering are not widely known. Perhaps few members of the Church realize that Elder Taylor was homebound for several weeks afterward, requiring the Twelve to meet in council at his home as they dealt with the effects and aftermath of the martyrdom.

Although an understanding of these things is not necessary for salvation, this knowledge can, nevertheless, have a tremendously positive effect in building testimonies. A complete knowledge of the events and the contexts in which they occurred leads to the assurance and testimony that the Lord's hand was in the entire affair and that He did *not* abandon Joseph and Hyrum in their most desperate circumstances. These assurances help confirm the certainty of Joseph Smith's mission as the prophet of the Restoration. An understanding of the miraculous events that occurred in Elder Taylor's wounding and preservation can also assist in building faith and testimony.

Fortunately, a record of the martyrdom was ultimately prepared and preserved. Its preparation was interwoven with the compilation of *History of The Church of Jesus Christ of Latter-day Saints* (hereafter referred to as *History*). But it wasn't until several years after the removal of the Church to the Rocky Mountains that the *History* associated with the Nauvoo era, and consequently, the record of the martyrdom was completed.[3] The great migration from Nauvoo to the valley of the Great Salt Lake suspended almost all such activities. Not until the mid-1850s—a decade later—did that work on the *History* resume. The untimely death of Elder Willard Richards, Church historian, in 1854, triggered renewed commitment to the task of completing the *History,* and that task fell upon Elder George A. Smith. Elder Smith soon began collecting information from anyone who had been with Joseph and Hyrum during their last days at Carthage, including such people as Edward A. Bedell, aide-de-camp to Governor Ford (and by then the Utah Indian agent), Cyrus Wheelock, Dan Jones, and others.

But for Elder Smith the task of extracting and integrating pertinent information from those sources into a readable history was "long, tedious, and difficult." He reported that even an hour's work on the project resulted in a headache.[4] His charge to complete the *History* was interrupted in 1856 when he was appointed to assist in drafting a Utah state constitution. Further, on 26 March 1856 he was appointed, along with Elder John Taylor, to present a petition for Utah statehood to the United States Congress. Consequently, and perhaps to his relief, Elder Smith took a sabbatical from the historian's office to fulfill these other duties. Little did he know that in this temporary change of venue a partial solution to his struggles with the *History* would emerge, one with which he would be intimately involved.

At the time, Elder Taylor was serving a mission on the East Coast. As editor and publisher of the New York City newspaper *The Mormon* and also as president of the Eastern States Mission of the Church, he joined Elder Smith in Washington, D.C., where the two labored together during the summer of 1856 to approach members of Congress with the objective of having a bill introduced for Utah's admission to the Union.

In the April 1856 general conference of the Church, Elder Wilford Woodruff had been named assistant Church historian. Thus, in Elder Smith's absence, the primary duties of documenting and recording the events of the martyrdom in the *History* fell on Elder Woodruff. In reviewing the available materials as he embarked on the assignment, he found significant gaps and contradictions and soon realized that some other source must be accessed, one that was more reliable than any other. In his mind, only an "eye and ear witness" to the events would suffice in supplying most of the missing pieces and resolutions to perceived inaccuracies, and there was only one such source on the entire face of the earth, and that source was Elder John Taylor.[5]

Why Elder Smith had not previously contacted Elder Taylor for this purpose is somewhat puzzling. Elder Taylor had been a leading participant in the events that culminated in the martyrdom. Indeed, aside from Joseph and Hyrum, no one had experienced the effects of the martyrdom more intimately. Knowing that Elder Taylor possessed a singular knowledge of the martyrdom, Elder Woodruff wrote to him on 30 June 1856, placing a significant responsibility on Elder Taylor's shoulders:

Dear Brother:

We are very busy writing the history of the latter days of Joseph, and we have a great many conflicting statements on the subject, which renders it necessary for me to call in the aid of an eye and ear witness to enable me to do justice to it. You are the only person on earth who can render me this assistance. I shall therefore feel obliged if you would take the earliest opportunity to sit down with your Hon. Colleague the Chief Historian to write out an account of all the circumstances relating to this subject which came under your immediate observation.[6]

Elder Woodruff then set forth a lengthy series of issues upon which he desired clarification, including such detailed questions as who offered the evening prayers at the jail, who requested Elder Taylor to sing "A Poor Wayfaring Man of Grief," and who washed the bodies of Joseph and Hyrum in Carthage. He left no question as to what he wanted Elder Taylor to address:

> I want you to describe the scenes in the jail with *great care and minuteness;* for as I said before you are the *only* man on earth who can do it [emphasis added].[7]

To support and assist Elder Taylor in this assignment, Elder Woodruff wrote to Elder Smith, who was then laboring with Elder Taylor in Washington, D.C., on the Utah statehood petition. He also wrote to Dr. John M. Bernhisel (another Carthage witness then serving as a Utah Territory delegate to Congress) and requested him to sit in council with Elders Taylor and Smith to support the effort. Placing an urgency on Elder Smith, Elder Woodruff stated:

> I hope Bro. Smith you will lose no time in attending to this matter, as the History must in a manner remain open until we can get your answer; we wish you to question brothers Taylor and Bernhisel upon every point that you deem necessary for the history, and forward to us immediately.[8]

Elder Taylor accepted the responsibility that had been placed on his shoulders. And it must have seemed a daunting one. The martyrdom had occurred twelve years previously. Perhaps he doubted the veracity of his memory or his ability to properly preserve the final scenes of Joseph's life in a way that would convey the honor, respect, and admiration he held for his intimate friend, mentor, and founder of The Church of Jesus Christ of Latter-day Saints. To avoid interruptions and to devote his full time to writing, he and Elder Smith retreated to the comparatively rural Westport, Connecticut, home of Westport branch president Ebenezer R. Young. Elders Taylor and Smith concluded, as suggested by Elder Woodruff, that the most efficient and effective way to accomplish their assignment was for Elder Taylor to write a narrative which addressed the issues Elder Smith had been charged to discuss with him. In his character as an editor and publisher, Elder Taylor prepared a lengthy document to settle any question about what happened in Carthage. He labored for several weeks on the project, assisted by Elder Smith and Dr. Bernhisel. After the project had come to a close, Elder Smith reported to Brigham Young:

> [Elder Taylor] has made a rough draft entirely from memory. . . . It will be the most complete account of the martyrdom of the Prophet yet produced, or that probably ever will be, as it comes from personal observation & will read extremely well, as it is given in his natural style, plain and unvarnished.[9]

The draft that Elder Taylor forwarded to the historian's office is dated 23 August 1856, at Branch Mills, Westport, Connecticut.

Because it was so comprehensive, Elder Taylor's manuscript became the measuring stick to gauge the accuracy of the other sources available to the Church historian regarding the martyrdom. The original manuscript, in his own pen, totals sixty-nine handwritten pages. His discourse is remarkable in language, tone, and content as he recounts not only the motivations and movements of the parties involved at the time, but also the details of many of the Prophet's last utterances, including the lengthy conversations in which Joseph engaged Illinois Governor Thomas Ford. Elder Taylor leaves the reader with no small impression of what Joseph, himself, and others experienced as they encountered and confronted what were bitter, and ultimately deadly, enemies. The Martyrdom Manuscript provides a stirring account that could only be told by one who was fully immersed in the councils and events that transpired.

Despite the fact that the Martyrdom Manuscript was written as a historical document, it is also intensely personal, and reading it kindles numerous emotions. The reader experiences Elder Taylor's deep regard for Joseph and his prophetic calling, his disgust and antipathy toward the persecuting "Gentiles," his agony and suffering from his wounds, and the deep loneliness and detachment associated with losing his prophet and his friend.

The first complete copy of the Martyrdom Manuscript that appeared in public surfaced in a book that was printed in 1862 by Richard F. Burton, a Victorian Englishman and adventure traveler whose profession it was to visit exotic places of the world and publish vivid portrayals of his journeys through the medium of books. In the 1860s Mormons were considered a great curiosity in England. Since the martyrdom and the amazing exodus to the desert, the Church had flourished nearly beyond belief. The English press continued to give the Church publicity. The success of the Church, combined with circulating reports (both true and false) regarding its leadership, and the preeminence of figures like Brigham Young, Heber C. Kimball, John Taylor, and others made the Salt Lake Valley a destination of numerous writers, of which Richard F. Burton was only one.

Burton visited Salt Lake City in the summer of 1860 and stayed for about three weeks, mingling with the Saints and Church leaders. Among all the writers who visited Great Salt Lake City, Burton took a distinct interest in Elder Taylor and his history. Realizing, perhaps, that Elder Taylor was a fellow Englishman by birth, and learning that he was a witness to the martyrdom in Carthage, Burton desired to meet him. The initial encounter occurred somewhat by chance, and the Englishman conversed with Elder Taylor for several minutes before realizing who he was. Burton's description of that introduction and the interchange that occurred between them is amusing. The exchange ultimately resulted in Elder Taylor's inviting Burton to accompany him on Church business to the Sugar House ward, offering further opportunity for the two to continue their exchange. In describing these events, Burton reveals his esteem for John Taylor and the Martyrdom Manuscript. Elder Taylor supplied him with a copy of the manuscript at some point during Burton's visit to Salt Lake City. To provide a glimpse of the interaction between John Taylor and Richard Burton, and a rare description of John Taylor's person through the eyes of an "outsider," I include a copy of Burton's account (along with his own footnotes) of the chance meeting substantially in its entirety with his original spelling intact:

> On the evening of 3rd September, whilst sauntering about the square in which a train of twenty-three wagons had just bivouacked: amongst the many others to whom Mr. S. introduced me, was the Apostle John Taylor, the "Champion of Rights," Speaker in the House, and whilome editor. I had heard of him from the best authorities as a man so morose and averse to Gentiles, "who made the healing virtue depart out of him," that it would be advisable to avoid his "fierceness." The *véridique* Mr. Austin Ward, describes him as "an old man deformed and crippled," and Mrs. Ferris as a "heavy dark-coloured beetle-browed man." Of course, I could not recognise him from these descriptions; —a stout, good-looking somewhat elderly personage, with a kindly grey eye, pleasant expression, and a forehead of the superior order; he talked of Westmoreland his birthplace, and of his European travels for a time, till the subject of Carthage coming upon the *tapis,* I suspected who my interlocutor was. Mr. S. burst out laughing when he heard my mistake, and I explained the reason to the Apostle, who laughed as heartily. Wishing to see more of him, I accompanied him in the carriage to the Sugar House Ward, where he was bound on business, and *chemin faisant* we had a long talk. He pointed out to me on the left the mouths of the several kanyons, and informed me that the City Creek and the Red Buttes on the north-east, and the Emigration, Parley's, Mill Creek, Great Cottonwood and Little Cottonwood kanyons to the east and

southeast, all head together in two points, thus enabling troops and provisions to be easily and readily concentrated for the defence of the eastern approaches. When talking about the probability of gold digging being developed near Gr. S. L. City, he said that the Mormons are aware of that, but that they look upon agriculture as their real wealth. Arriving at the tall gaunt Sugar House—its occupation is gone whilst the name remains—we examined the machinery employed in making threshing and wool-carding machines, flanges, wheels, cranks, and similar necessaries. . . . On our return, we resumed the subject of the massacre at Carthage, in which it will be remembered, Mr. John Taylor was severely wounded and escaped by a miracle as it were. I told him openly that there must have been some cause for the furious proceedings of the people in Illinois, Missouri, and other places against the Latter-Day Saints; that even those who had extended hospitality to them ended by hating and expelling them, and accusing them of all possible iniquities, especially of horse-thieving, forgery, larceny, and offences against property which on the border are never pardoned—was this smoke quite without fire? He heard me courteously and in perfect temper, replied that no one claimed immaculateness for the Mormons; that the net cast into the sea brought forth evil as well as good fish, and that the Prophet was one of the labourers sent into the vineyard at the eleventh hour. At the same time that when the New Faith was stoutly struggling into existence, it was the object of detraction, odium, persecution—so, said Mr. Taylor, were the Christians in the days of Nero—that the border ruffians, forgers, horse-thieves, and other vile fellows followed the Mormons wherever they went; and finally that every fraud and crime was charged upon those whom the populace were disposed by desire for confiscation's sake to believe guilty. Besides the theologic odium there was also the political: the Saints would vote for their favourite candidates, consequently they were never without enemies. He quoted the Mormon rules:—1. Worship what you like. 2. Leave your neighbour alone. 3. Vote for whom you please; and compared their troubles to the Western, or, as it is popularly called the Whiskey insurrection in 1794, whose "dreadful night" is still remembered in Pennsylvania. Mr. Taylor remarked that the Saints had been treated by the United States as the colonies had been treated by the Crown. . . . I heard for the first time this view of the question, and subsequently obtained from the Apostle a manuscript account, written *in extenso,* of his experience and his sufferings. It has been transferred in its integrity to Appendix No. 3.—the length forbidding its insertion in the text: a tone of candour, simplicity and honesty, renders it highly attractive.

Thus the Martyrdom Manuscript was introduced to the world. And Richard Burton was not the only one who held the Martyrdom Manuscript in high esteem. In editing the *History* for publication in its present seven-volume format in the early 1900s, Elder B. H. Roberts studied the text carefully and included it in the *History* in its entirety. Elder Roberts made the following assessment of the Manuscript:

[The manuscript] is a review and commentary of the period [of the Martyrdom] of highest value, a statesman-like paper, a document of highest historical value of the time; and one marvels at the high tone with which the document is planned. . . . In my study of historical documents . . . without exception I can say that I have examined nothing that is equal in spirit and justice to this review by [Elder] Taylor. . . . It deserves to live forever.[10]

Although the Martyrdom Manuscript is preserved in the *History,* it has, nevertheless, remained relatively obscure.[11] The purpose of this volume is to help fulfill Elder Roberts's determination in a broader context. How can any document live unless it is alive in the minds and hearts of the people? With Elder Roberts's determination in mind, this work is placed more openly before the Church. In preparing this volume, I first gained access to the manuscript version found in Richard Burton's *City of the Saints,* as it was the original publication. As indicated, however, the Martyrdom Manuscript has appeared elsewhere, most notably *History of The Church of Jesus Christ of Latter-day Saints,* compiled by B. H. Roberts. Accordingly, the account that follows has been correlated with the version in the *History* and discrepancies resolved by relying on that version. In some cases, the manuscript was correlated to the original handwritten version found in the Church Archives as well.

In editing the manuscript for publication in this work, I felt the need to divide the lengthy account into chapters; hence, the chapter headings are mine. Original wording, spellings, and punctuation have been preserved unless otherwise noted. Notes to the manuscript, found in chapter

15, have been included from three sources. Richard Burton inserted his own notes; B. H. Roberts also included notes for clarification; and I have added several as well. The source of the note is stipulated in each insert. In all cases, notes are included to add to the harmony of the overall presentation. What follows, then, is John Taylor's eye-witness account of the martyrdom of Joseph Smith.

NOTES

1. D&C 109:73.

2. Joseph Smith—History 1:33.

3. For a comprehensive analysis of the compiling of the history of the martyrdom, see Dean C. Jessee, "Return to Carthage: Writing the History of Joseph Smith's Martyrdom," *Journal of Mormon History* 8 (1981):3–19.

4. Letters from George A. Smith to C. C. Waller, 31 July 1855, and to John Lyman [Smith], 30 September 1855. Historian's Office Letterbook 1, p. 230, and Historian's Office Journal, 26 August 1854.

5. Elder Woodruff contacted other individuals who also supplied their own accounts of the incident, but none was as comprehensive or as lengthy as Elder Taylor's.

6. Letter from Wilford Woodruff to John Taylor, 30 June 1856, Historian's Office Letterbook 1, pp. 315–19.

7. Ibid.

8. Letter from Wilford Woodruff to George A. Smith, 30 June 1856, Historian's Office Letterbook 1, p. 319.

9. Letter from George A. Smith to Brigham Young, 19 September 1856, LDS Church Archives.

10. See B. H. Roberts, ed., *History of The Church of Jesus Christ of Latter-day Saints,* 7 vols. (Salt Lake City: Deseret News Press, 1930), 7:xxii.

11. The Manuscript has appeared in other places. Daniel Tyler, third sergeant of Company C of the Mormon Battalion, prepared a history of the Mormon Battalion that was published in 1881. To provide the background under which the Battalion was mustered in 1846, Tyler requested permission from John Taylor (then President of the Church) that the Manuscript be

included as an introductory chapter to the Battalion's history (see Daniel Tyler, *A Concise History of the Mormon Battalion in the Mexican War, 1846–1848* [1881; reprinted Salt Lake City: Publishers Press, 1996]). President Taylor agreed. The Manuscript also appeared in N. B. Lundwall, *The Fate of the Persecutors of the Prophet Joseph Smith* (Salt Lake City: Bookcraft, 1952).

Part 2

———

JOHN TAYLOR'S
ACCOUNT

Chapter 1

INTRODUCTION

———

Being requested by Elders George A. Smith and Wilford Woodruff, Church Historians, to write an account of events that transpired before, and took place at the time of the martyrdom of Joseph Smith, in Carthage jail, in Hancock county, state of Illinois, I write the following, principally from memory, not having access at this time to any public documents relative thereto, farther than a few desultory items contained in Ford's *History of Illinois.* I must also acknowledge myself considerably indebted to George A. Smith, who was with me when I wrote it, and who, although not there at the time of the bloody transaction, yet, from conversing with several persons who were in the capacity of Church Historians, and aided by an excellent memory, has rendered me a considerable service.

These and the few items contained in the note at the end of this account is all the aid I have had. I would farther add that the items contained in the letter, in relation to dates especially, may be considered strictly correct.

After having written the whole, I read it over to the Hon. J. M. Bernhisel, who with one or two slight alterations, pronounced it strictly correct. Brother Bernhisel was present most of the time. I am afraid that, from the length of time that has transpired since the occurrence, and having to rely almost exclusively upon my memory, there may be some slight inaccuracies, but I believe that in general it is strictly correct. As I figured in those transactions from the commencement to the end, they left no slight impression on my mind.

Chapter 2

CONDITIONS AND GRIEVANCES

———

In the year 1844, a very great excitement prevailed in some parts of Hancock, Brown, and other neighboring counties of Illinois, in relation to the "Mormons", [Editor's note: Here and elsewhere, irregular punctuation has been preserved] and a spirit of vindictive hatred and persecution was exhibited among the people, which was manifested in the most bitter and acrimonious language, as well as by acts of hostility and violence, frequently threatening the destruction of the citizens of Nauvoo and vicinity, and utter annihilation of the "Mormons" and "Mormonism", and in some instances breaking out in the most violent acts of ruffianly barbarity. Persons were kidnapped, whipped, persecuted, and falsely accused of various crimes; their cattle and houses injured, destroyed, or stolen; vexatious prosecutions were instituted to harass and annoy. In some remote neighborhoods they were expelled from their homes without redress, and in others violence was threatened to their persons and properties, while in others every kind of insult and indignity were heaped upon them, to induce them to abandon their homes, the county, or the state.

These annoyances, prosecutions, and persecutions were instigated through different agencies and by various classes of men, actuated by different motives, but all uniting in the one object—prosecution, persecution, and extermination of the saints.

There were a number of wicked and corrupt men living in Nauvoo and its vicinity, who had belonged to the church, but whose conduct was incompatible with the gospel; they were accordingly dealt with by the church and severed from its communion. Some of these had been prominent members, and held official stations, either in the city or church. Among these were John C. Bennett, formerly mayor; William Law, counselor to Joseph Smith; Wilson Law, his natural brother, and general in the Nauvoo Legion; Dr. R. D. Foster, a man of some property, but with a very bad reputation; Francis and Chauncey Higbee, the latter a young lawyer, and both sons of a respectable and honored man in the church, known as Judge Elias Higbee, who died about twelve months before.

Besides these, there were a great many apostates, both in the city and county, of less notoriety, who for their delinquencies, had been expelled from the church. John C. Bennett and Francis and Chauncey Higbee were cut off from the church; the former was also cashiered from his generalship for the most flagrant acts of seduction and adultery; and the developments in their cases were so scandalous that the high council, before whom they were tried, had to sit with closed doors.

William Law, although counselor to Joseph, was found to be his most bitter foe and maligner, and to hold intercourse [it was alleged], contrary to all law, in his own house, with a young lady resident with him; and it was afterwards proved that he had conspired with some Missourians, to take Joseph Smith's life, and [the Prophet] was only saved by Josiah Arnold and Daniel Garn, who, being on guard at his house, prevented the assassins from seeing him. Yet, although having murder in his heart, his manners were generally courteous and mild, and he was well calculated to deceive.

General Wilson Law was cut off from the church for seduction, falsehood, and defamation; both the above were also court-martialed by the Nauvoo Legion and expelled. Foster was also cut off I believe, for dishonesty, fraud, and falsehood. I know he was eminently guilty of the whole, but whether these were the specific charges or not, I don't know, but I do know that he was a notoriously wicked and corrupt man.

Besides the above characters and "Mormonic" apostates, there were other three parties. The first of these may be called religionists, the second politicians, and the third counterfeiters, blacklegs, horse thieves, and cutthroats.

The religious party were chagrined and maddened because "Mormonism" came in contact with their religion, and they could not oppose it from the scriptures. Thus like the ancient Jews, when enraged at the exhibition of their follies and hypocrisies by Jesus and his Apostles, so these were infuriated against the "Mormons" because of their discomfiture by them; and instead of owning the truth and rejoicing in it, they were ready to gnash upon them with their teeth, and to persecute the believers in principles which they could not disprove.

The political party were those who were of opposite politics to us. There were always two parties, the whigs and democrats, and we could not vote for one without offending the other, and it not unfrequently happened that candidates for office would place the issue of their election upon opposition to the "Mormons", in order to gain political influence from religious prejudice, in which case the "Mormons" were compelled, in self-defense, to vote against them, which resulted almost invariably against our opponents. This made them angry; and although it was of their own making, and the "Mormons" could not be expected to do otherwise, yet they raged on account of their discomfiture, and sought to wreak their fury on the "Mormons". As an instance of the above, when Joseph Duncan was candidate for office of governor of Illinois, he pledged himself to his party that, if he could be elected, he would exterminate or drive the "Mormons" from the state.[1] The consequence was that Governor Ford was elected. The whigs, seeing that they had been out-generaled by the democrats in securing the "Mormon" vote, became seriously alarmed, and sought to repair their disaster by raising a kind of crusade against the people. The whig newspapers teemed with accounts of the wonders and enormities of Nauvoo, and of the awful wickedness of a party which could consent to receive the support of such miscreants. Governor Duncan, who was really a brave, honest man, and who had nothing to do with getting the "Mormon" charters passed through the legislature, took the stump on this subject in good earnest, and expected to be elected governor almost on this question alone.

The third party, composed of counterfeiters, blacklegs, horse thieves, and cutthroats, were a pack of scoundrels that infested the whole of the western country at that time. In some districts their influence was so great as to control important state and county offices. On this subject Governor Ford has the following:—

> Then, again, the northern part of the State was not destitute of its organized bands of rogues, engaged in murders, robberies, horse-stealing, and in making and passing counterfeit money. These rogues were scattered all over the north, but the most of them were located in the counties of Ogle, Winnebago, Lee, and De Kalb.
>
> In the county of Ogle they were so numerous, strong, and well organized, that they could not be convicted for their crimes. By getting some of their numbers on the juries, by producing a host of witnesses to sustain their defense by perjured evidence, and by changing the venue of one county to another, by continuances from term to term, and by the inability of witnesses to attend from time to time at distant and foreign counties, they most generally managed to be acquitted.[2]

There was a combination of horse thieves extending from Galena to Alton. There were counterfeiters engaged in merchandizing, trading, and storekeeping in most of the cities and villages, and in some districts, I have been credibly informed by men to whom they have disclosed their secrets; the judges, sheriffs, constables, and jailors, as well as professional men, were more or less associated with

them. These had in their employ the most reckless, abandoned wretches, who stood ready to carry into effect the
most desperate enterprises, and were careless alike of
human life and property. Their object in persecuting the
"Mormons" was in part to cover their own rascality, and in
part to prevent them from exposing and prosecuting them;
but the principal reason was plunder, believing that if they
[the "Mormons"] could be removed or driven, they would
be made fat on "Mormon" spoils, besides having in the
deserted city a good asylum for the prosecution of their diabolical pursuits.

This conglomeration of apostate "Mormons", religious
bigots, political fanatics, and blacklegs, all united their
forces against the "Mormons", and organized themselves
into a party, denominated "anti-Mormons". Some of them,
we have reason to believe, joined the church in order to
cover their nefarious practices, and when they were
expelled for their unrighteousness only raged with greater
violence. They circulated every kind of falsehood that they
could collect or manufacture against the "Mormons". They
also had a paper to assist them in their infamous designs,
called the *Warsaw Signal,* edited by a Mr. Thomas Sharp, a
violent and unprincipled man, who shrunk not from any
enormity. The anti-"Mormons" had public meetings, which
were very numerously attended, where they passed resolutions of the most violent and inflammatory kind, threatening to drive, expel and exterminate the "Mormons" from
the state, at the same time accusing them of every evil in the
vocabulary of crime.

They appointed their meetings in various parts of

Hancock, McDonough, and other counties, which soon resulted in the organization of armed mobs, under the direction of officers who reported to their headquarters, and the reports of which were published in the anti-"Mormon paper," and circulated through the adjoining counties. We also published in the *Times and Seasons* and the *Nauvoo Neighbour* (two papers published and edited by me at that time), an account, not only of their proceedings, but our own. But such was the hostile feeling, so well arranged their plans, and so desperate and lawless their measures, that it was with the greatest difficulty that we could get our papers circulated; they were destroyed by postmasters and others, and scarcely ever arrived at the place of their destination, so that a great many of the people, who would have been otherwise peaceable, were excited by their misrepresentations, and instigated to join their hostile or predatory bands.

NOTES

1. See his remarks as contained in Ford's *History of Illinois,* p. 269 [John Taylor's note; hereafter, all such identified as JT].

2. Ford's *History of Illinois,* p. 246 [JT].

The trial of the nine accused assassins also failed to convict anyone for the murders of Joseph and Hyrum Smith—see Dallin H. Oaks and M. S. Hill, *Carthage Conspiracy* (Urbana: University of Illinois Press, 1975) [Mark Taylor's note; hereafter, all such identified as MT].

Chapter 3

THE *EXPOSITOR*

———

Emboldened by the acts of those outside, the apostate "Mormons", associated with others, commenced the publication of a libellous paper in Nauvoo, called the *Nauvoo Expositor.* This paper not only reprinted from the others, but put in circulation the most libellous, false, and infamous reports concerning the citizens of Nauvoo, and especially the ladies. It was, however, no sooner put in circulation, than the indignation of the whole community was aroused; so much so, that they threatened its annihilation; and I do not believe that in any other city in the United States, if the same charges had been made against the citizens, it would have been permitted to remain one day. As it was among us, under these circumstances, it was thought best to convene the city council to take into consideration the adoption of some measures for its removal, as it was deemed better that this should be done legally than illegally. Joseph Smith, therefore, who was mayor, convened the city council for that purpose; the paper was introduced and read, and the subject examined. All, or nearly all present, expressed their indignation at the course taken by the

Expositor, which was owned by some of the aforesaid apostates, associated with one or two others. Wilson Law, Dr.
Foster, Charles Ivins and the Higbees before referred to,
some lawyers, storekeepers, and others in Nauvoo who
were not "Mormons", together with the anti-"Mormons"
outside the city, sustained it. The calculation was, by false
statements, to unsettle the minds of many in the city, and to
form combinations there similar to the anti-"Mormon"
associations outside of the city. Various attempts had
heretofore been made by the party to annoy and irritate the
citizens of Nauvoo; false accusations had been made, vexatious lawsuits instituted, threats made, and various devices
resorted to, to influence the public mind, and, if possible,
to provoke us to the commission of some overt act that
might make us amenable to the law. With a perfect knowledge, therefore, of the designs of these infernal scoundrels
who were in our midst, as well of those who surrounded us,
the city council entered upon an investigation of the matter.
They felt that they were in a critical position, and that any
move made for the abating of that press would be looked
upon, or at least represented, as a direct attack upon the liberty of speech, and that, so far from displeasing our enemies, it would be looked upon by them as one of the best
circumstances that could transpire to assist them in the
nefarious and bloody designs. Being a member of the city
council, I well remember the feeling of responsibility that
seemed to rest upon all present; nor shall I soon forget the
bold, manly, independent expressions of Joseph Smith on
that occasion in relation to this matter. He exhibited in
glowing colors the meanness, corruption and ultimate

designs of the anti-"Mormons"; their despicable characters and ungodly influences, especially of those who were in our midst. He told of the responsibility that rested upon us, as guardians of the public interest, to stand up in the defense of the injured and oppressed, to stem the current of corruption, and as men and saints, to put a stop to this flagrant outrage upon this people's rights.

He stated that no man was a stronger advocate for the liberty of the speech and of the press than himself; yet, when this noble gift is utterly prostituted and abused, as in the present instance, it loses all claim to our respect, and becomes as great an agent for evil as it can possibly be for good; and notwithstanding the apparent advantage we should give our enemies by this act, yet it behooved us, as men, to act independent of all secondary influences, to perform the part of men of enlarged minds, and boldly and fearlessly to discharge the duties devolving upon us by declaring as a nuisance, and removing this filthy, libellous, and seditious sheet from our midst.

The subject was discussed in various forms, and after the remarks made by the mayor, every one seemed to be waiting for some one else to speak.

After a considerable pause, I arose and expressed my feelings frankly, as Joseph had done, and numbers of others followed in the same strain; and I think, but am not certain, that I made a motion for the removal of that press as a nuisance. This motion was finally put, and carried by all but one; and he conceded that the measure was just, but abstained through fear.

Several of the members of the city council were not in the church. The following is the bill referred to:—

Bill for Removing of the Press of the "Nauvoo Expositor."

Resolved by the city council of the city of Nauvoo, that the printing office, from whence issues the *Nauvoo Expositor,* is a public nuisance; and also of said *Nauvoo Expositors* which may be or exist in said establishment; and the mayor is instructed to cause said establishment and papers to be removed without delay, in such manner as he shall direct.

Passed June 10th, 1844.

W. RICHARDS, Recorder
GEO. W. HARRIS, President, *pro tem.*[1]

After the passage of the bill, the marshal, John P. Green, was ordered to abate or remove, which he forthwith proceeded to do by summoning a posse of men for that purpose. The press was removed or broken, I don't remember which, by the marshal, and the types scattered in the street.

This seemed to be one of those extreme cases that require extreme measures, as the press was still proceeding in its inflammatory course. It was feared that, as it was almost universally execrated, should it continue longer, an indignant people might commit some overt act which might lead to serious consequences, and that it was better to use legal than illegal means.

This, as was foreseen, was the very course our enemies wished us to pursue, as it afforded them an opportunity of circulating a very plausible story about the "Mormons" being opposed to the liberty of the press and of free speech, which they were not slow to avail themselves of. Stories were fabricated, and facts perverted; false statements were made, and this act brought in as an example to sustain the whole of their fabrications; and, as if inspired by satan, they labored with an energy and zeal worthy of a better cause. They had runners to circulate their reports, not only through Hancock County, but in all the surrounding counties. These reports were communicated to their anti-"Mormon" societies, and these societies circulated them in their several districts. The anti-"Mormon" paper, the *Warsaw Signal,* was filled with inflammatory articles and misrepresentations in relation to us, and especially to this act of destroying the press. We were represented as a horde of lawless ruffians and brigands, anti-American and anti-republican, steeped in crime and iniquity, opposed to freedom of speech and of the press, and all the rights and immunities of a free and enlightened people; that neither person nor property were secure, that we had designs upon the citizens of Illinois and of the United States, and the people were called upon to rise *en masse,* and put us down, drive us away, or exterminate us as a pest to society, and alike dangerous to our neighbors, the state, and the commonwealth.

These statements were extensively copied and circulated throughout the United States. A true statement of the facts in question was published by us both in the *Times and Seasons* and the *Nauvoo Neighbour;* but it was found impossible to circulate them in the immediate counties, as they were destroyed at the post offices or otherwise by the agents of the anti-"Mormons", and, in order to get the mail to go

abroad, I had to send the papers a distance of thirty or forty
miles from Nauvoo, and sometimes to St. Louis (upward of
two hundred miles), to insure their proceeding on their
route, and then one-half or two-thirds of the papers never
reached the place of destination, being intercepted or
destroyed by our enemies.

These false reports stirred up the community around,
of whom many, on account of religious prejudice, were easily instigated to join the anti-"Mormons", and embark in
any crusade that might be undertaken against us; hence
their ranks swelled in numbers, and new organizations were
formed, meetings were held, resolutions passed, and men
and means volunteered for the extirpation of the
"Mormons".

On these points Governor Ford writes:

These also were the active men in blowing up the
fury of the people, in hopes that a popular movement
might be set on foot, which would result in the expulsion or extermination of the "Mormon" voters. For this
purpose public meetings had been called, inflammatory
speeches had been made, exaggerated reports had been
extensively circulated, committees had been appointed,
who rode night and day to spread the reports and
solicit the aid of neighboring counties, and at a public
meeting at Warsaw resolutions were passed to expel or
exterminate the "Mormon" population. This was not,
however, a movement which was unanimously con-
curred in. The county contained a goodly number of
inhabitants in favor of peace, or who at least desired to
be neutral in such a contest. These were stigmatized by
the name of "Jack-Mormons", and there were not a

few of the more furious exciters of the people who openly expressed their intention to involve them in the common expulsion or extermination.

A system of excitement and agitation was artfully planned and executed with tact. It consisted in spreading reports and rumors of the most fearful character. As examples:—On the morning before my arrival at Carthage, I was awakened at an early hour by the frightful report, which was asserted with confidence and apparent consternation, that the "Mormons" had already commenced the work of burning, destruction, and murder, and that every man capable of bearing arms was instantly wanted at Carthage for the protection of the county.

We lost no time in starting, but when we arrived at Carthage we could hear no more concerning this story. Again, during the few days that the militia were encamped at Carthage, frequent applications were made to me to send a force here, and a force there, and a force all about the country, to prevent murders, robberies, and larcenies which, it was said, were threatened by the "Mormons". No such forces were sent, nor were any such offenses committed at that time, except the stealing of some provisions, and there was never the least proof that this was done by a "Mormon". Again, on my late visit to Hancock county, I was informed by some of their violent enemies that the larcenies of the "Mormons" had become unusually numerous and insufferable.

They admitted that but little had been done in this way in their immediate vicinity, but they insisted that sixteen horses had been stolen by the "Mormons" in

one night near Lima, and upon inquiry, was told that
no horses had been stolen in that neighborhood, but
that sixteen horses had been stolen in one night in
Hancock county. This last informant being told of the
Hancock story, again changed the venue to another distant settlement in the northern edge of Adams.[2]

In the meantime legal proceedings were instituted
against the members of the city council of Nauvoo. A writ,
here subjoined, was issued upon the affidavit of the Laws,
Fosters, Higbees, and Ivins, by Mr. Morrison, a justice of
the peace in Carthage, and the county seat of Hancock, and
put into the hands of one David Bettisworth, a constable of
the same place.

Writ issued upon affidavit by Thomas Morrison, J.P.,
State of Illinois,

Hancock County, s.s.

The people of the state of Illinois, to all constables,
sheriffs, and coroners of said State, greeting:

Whereas complaint hath been made before me,
one of the justices of the peace in and for the county of
Hancock, aforesaid, upon the oath of Francis M.
Higbee, of the said county, that Joseph Smith, Samuel
Bennett, John Taylor, William W. Phelps, Hyrum
Smith, John P. Green, Stephen Perry, Dimick B.
Huntington, Jonathan Dunham, Stephen Markham,
William Edwards, Jonathan Holmes, Jesse P. Harmon,
John Lytle, Joseph W. Coolidge, Harvey D. Redfield,
Porter Rockwell, and Levi Richards, of said county, did
on the 10th day of June instant, commit a riot at and
within the county aforesaid, wherein they with force
and violence broke into the printing office of the

Nauvoo Expositor, and unlawfully and with force burned and destroyed the printing press, type and fixtures of the same, being the property of William Law, Wilson Law, Charles Ivins, Francis M. Higbee, Chauncey L. Higbee, Robert D. Foster, and Charles A. Foster.

These are therefore to command you forthwith to apprehend the said Joseph Smith, Samuel Bennett, John Taylor, William W. Phelps, Hyrum Smith, John P. Green, Stephen Perry, Dimick B. Huntington, Jonathan Dunham, Stephen Markham, William Edwards, Jonathan Holmes, Jesse P. Harmon, John Lytle, Joseph W. Coolidge, Harvey D. Redfield, Porter Rockwell, and Levi Richards, and bring them before me, or some other justice of the peace, to answer the premises, and further to be dealt with according to law.

Given under my hand and seal at Carthage, in the county aforesaid, this 11th day of June, A.D., 1844.

[signed] THOMAS MORRISON, J.P. (Seal)[3]

The council did not refuse to attend to the legal proceedings in the case, but as the law of Illinois made it the privilege of the persons accused to go "or appear before the issuer of the writ, *or any other justice of peace*", they requested to be taken before another magistrate, either in the city of Nauvoo or at any reasonable distance out of it.

This the constable, who was a mobocrat, refused to do, and as this was our legal privilege, we refused to be dragged, contrary to law, a distance of eighteen miles, when at the same time we had reason to believe that an organized band of mobocrats were assembled for the purpose of extermination or murder, and among whom it would not be

safe to go without a superior force of armed men. A writ of
habeas corpus was called for, and issued by the municipal
court of Nauvoo, taking us out of the hands of Bettisworth,
and placing us in the charge of the city marshal. We went
before the municipal court, and were dismissed. Our refusal
to obey this illegal proceeding was by them construed into a
refusal to submit to law, and circulated as such, and the
people either did believe, or professed to believe, that we
were in open rebellion against the laws and the authorities
of the state. Hence mobs began to assemble, among which
all through the country inflammatory speeches were
made, exciting them to mobocracy and violence. Soon they
commenced their depredations in our outside settlements,
kidnaping some, and whipping and otherwise abusing
others.

The persons thus abused fled to Nauvoo as soon as
practicable, and related their injuries to Joseph Smith, then
mayor of the city, and lieutenant-general of the Nauvoo
Legion. They also went before magistrates, and made affidavits of what they had suffered, seen, and heard. These
affidavits, in connection with a copy of all our proceedings,
were forwarded by Joseph Smith to Mr. Ford, then governor of Illinois, with an expression of our desire to abide law,
and a request that the governor would instruct him how to
proceed in the case of arrival of an armed mob against the
city. The governor sent back instructions to Joseph Smith
that, as he was lieutenant-general of the Nauvoo Legion, it
was his duty to protect the city and surrounding country,
and issued orders to that effect. Upon the reception of these
orders Joseph Smith assembled the people of the city, and

laid before them the governor's instructions; he also convened the officers of the Nauvoo Legion for the purpose of conferring in relation to the best mode of defense. He also issued orders to the men to hold themselves in readiness in case of being called upon. On the following day General Joseph Smith, with his staff, the leading officers of the Legion, and some prominent strangers who were in our midst, made a survey of the outside boundaries of the city, which was very extensive, being about five miles up and down the river, and about two and a half back in the center, for the purpose of ascertaining the position of the ground, and the feasibility of defense, and to make all necessary arrangements in case of an attack.

It may be well here to remark that numbers of gentlemen, strangers to us, either came on purpose or were passing through Nauvoo, and, upon learning the position of things, expressed their indignation against our enemies, and avowed their readiness to assist us by their council or otherwise. It was some of these who assisted us in reconnoitering the city, and finding out its adaptability for defense, and how to protect it best against an armed force. The Legion was called together and drilled, and every means made use for defense. At the call of the officers, both old and young men came forward, both from the city and from the country, and they mustered to the number of about five thousand.

In the meantime our enemies were not idle in mustering their forces and committing depredations, nor had they been; it was, in fact, their gathering that called ours into existence; their forces continued to accumulate; they assumed a threatening attitude, and assembled in large bodies, armed and equipped for war, and threatened the destruction and extermination of the "Mormons".

An account of their outrages and assemblages was forwarded to Governor Ford almost daily; accompanied by affidavits furnished by eyewitnesses of their proceedings. Persons were also sent out to the counties around with pacific intentions, to give them an account of the true state of affairs, and to notify them of the feelings and dispositions of the people of Nauvoo, and thus, if possible, quell the excitement. In some of the more distant counties these men were very successful, and produced a salutary influence upon the minds of many intelligent and well-disposed men. In neighboring counties, however, where anti-"Mormon" influence prevailed, they produced little effect. At the same time guards were stationed around Nauvoo, and picket-guards in the distance. At length opposing forces gathered so near that more active measures were taken; reconnoitering parties were sent out, and the city proclaimed under martial law. Things now assumed a belligerent attitude, and persons passing through the city were questioned as to what they knew of the enemy, while passes were in some instances given to avoid difficulty with the guards. Joseph Smith continued to send on messengers to the governor (Philip B. Lewis and other messengers were sent). Samuel James, then residing at La Harpe, carried a message and dispatches to him, and in a day or two after Bishop Edward Hunter and others went again with fresh dispatches, representations, affidavits and instructions; but as the weather was excessively wet, the rivers swollen, and the bridges washed away in many places, it was with great difficulty that they proceeded on their journeys. As the mobocracy had at last attracted the governor's attention, he started in company with some others from Springfield to the scene of the trouble, and missed, I believe, both Brothers James and Hunter on the road, and, of course, did not see their documents. He came to Carthage, and made that place, which was a regular mobocratic den, his headquarters; as it was the countyseat, however, of Hancock county, that circumstance might, in a measure, justify his staying there.

To avoid the appearance of all hostility on our part, and to fulfill the law in every particular, at the suggestion of Judge Thomas, judge of that judicial district, who had come to Nauvoo at the time, and who stated that we had fulfilled the law, but, in order to satisfy all he would counsel us to go before Esquire Wells, who was not in our church, and have a hearing. We did so, and after a full hearing we were again dismissed.

NOTES

1. *Deseret News,* no. 29, 23 September 1857, p. 226 [JT].
2. Ford's *History of Illinois,* pp. 330–31 [JT].
3. *Deseret News,* no. 30, 30 September 1857, p. 233 [JT].

C h a p t e r 4

FORD'S FIASCO

———

The governor on the road collected forces, some of
whom were respectable, but on his arrival in the neighborhood of the difficulties, he received as militia all the
companies of the mob forces who united with him. After
his arrival at Carthage, he sent two gentlemen from there
to Nauvoo as a committee to wait upon General Joseph
Smith, informing him of the arrival of his excellency, with a
request that General Smith would send out a committee to
wait upon the governor and represent to him the state of
affairs in relation to the difficulties that then existed in the
county.

[MT: The governor's request came to Joseph Smith in
the form of this letter, which was reprinted in Burton's *City
of the Saints:*]

*Governor Ford's Letter to the Mayor and Common
Council of Nauvoo.*

Head Quarters, Carthage
June 21ˢᵗ, 1844

To the Hon. The Mayor and Common Council of the
City of Nauvoo.

GENTLEMEN,—Having heard of the excitement in this part of the country, and judging that my presence here might be necessary to preserve the peace and enforce the laws, I arrived at this place this morning. Both before and since my arrival, complaints of a grave character have been made to me of certain proceedings of your honorable body. As chief magistrate it is my duty to see that impartial justice shall be done, uninfluenced by the excitement here or in your city.

I think, before any decisive measure shall be adopted, that I ought to hear the allegations and defenses of all parties. By adopting this course I have some hope that the evils of war may be averted; and at any rate I will be enabled by it to understand the true merits of the present difficulties, and shape my course with reference to law and justice.

For these reasons I have to request that you will send out to me, at this place, one or more well-informed and discreet persons, who will be capable of laying before me your version of the matter, and of receiving from me such explanations and resolutions as may be determined on.

Colonel Elam S. Freeman will present you this note in the character of a herald from the governor. You will respect his character as such, and permit him to pass and repass free from molestation.

Your messengers are assured the protection in person and property, and will be returned to you safely.

I am, Gentlemen, with high considerations, most respectfully, your obedient servant.

THOMAS FORD,
Governor, and Commander-in-Chief[1]

We met this committee while we were reconnoitering the city to find out the best mode of defense as aforesaid. Dr. J. M. Bernhisel and myself were appointed as a committee by General Smith to wait upon the governor. Previous to going, however, we were furnished with affidavits and documents in relation both to our proceedings and those of the mob; in addition to the general history of the transaction, we took with us a duplicate of those documents which had been forwarded by Bishop Hunter, Brother James and others. We started from Nauvoo in company with the aforesaid gentlemen at about 7 o'clock on the evening of the 21st of June, and arrived at Carthage at about 11 P.M. We put up at the same hotel with the governor, kept by a Mr. Hamilton. On our arrival we found the governor in bed, but not so with the other inhabitants. The town was filled with a perfect set of rabble and rowdies, who, under the influence of bacchus, seemed to be holding a grand saturnalia, whooping, yelling and vociferating, as if bedlam had broken loose.

On our arrival at the hotel, and while supper was preparing, a man came to me, dressed as a soldier, and told me that a man named Daniel Garn had just been taken prisoner, and was about to be committed to jail, and wanted me to go bail for him. Believing this to be a ruse to get me out alone, and that some violence was intended, after consulting with Dr. Bernhisel, I told the man that I was well acquainted with Mr. Garn, that I knew him to be a gentleman, and did not believe that he had transgressed the law, and, moreover, that I considered it a very singular time to be holding courts and calling for security, particularly as the town was full of rowdyism.

I informed him that Dr. Bernhisel and myself would, if necessary, go bail for him in the morning, but that we did not feel ourselves safe among such a set at that late hour of the night.

After supper, on retiring to our room, we had to pass through another, which was separated from ours only by a board partition, the beds in each room being placed side by side, with the exception of this fragile partition. On the bed that was in the room which we passed through I discovered a man by the name of Jackson, a desperate character, and a reputed, notorious cutthroat and murderer. I hinted to the doctor that things looked rather suspicious, and looked to see that my arms were in order. The doctor and I occupied one bed. We had scarcely laid down when a knock at the door, accompanied by a voice announced the approach of Chauncey Higbee, the young lawyer and apostate before referred to.

He addressed himself to the doctor, and stated that the object of his visit was to obtain the release of Daniel Garn; that Garn he believed to be an honest man; that if he had done anything wrong, it was through improper counsel, and that it was a pity that he should be incarcerated, particularly when he could be so easily released; he urged the doctor, as a friend, not to leave so good a man in such an unpleasant situation; he finally prevailed upon the doctor to go and give bail, assuring him that on his giving bail Garn would be immediately dismissed.

During this conversation I did not say a word.

Higbee left the doctor to dress, with the intention of returning and taking him to the court. As soon as Higbee had left, I told the doctor that he had better not go; that I believed this affair was all a ruse to get us separated; that they knew we had documents with us from General Smith to show to the governor; that I believed their object was to get in possession of those papers, and, perhaps, when they had separated us, to murder one or both. The doctor, who was actuated by the best of motives in yielding to the assumed solicitude of Higbee, coincided with my views; he then went to Higbee and told him that he had concluded not to go that night, but that he and I would both wait upon the justice and Mr. Garn in the morning.

That night I lay awake with my pistols under my pillow, waiting for any emergency. Nothing more occurred during the night. In the morning we arose early, and after breakfast sought an interview with the governor, and were told that we could have an audience, I think, at 10 o'clock. In the meantime we called upon Mr. Smith, a justice of the peace, who had Mr. Garn in charge. We represented that we had been called upon the night before by two different parties to go bail for a Mr. Daniel Garn, whom we were informed he had in custody, and that, believing Mr. Garn to be an honest man, we had come now for that purpose, and were prepared to enter into recognizance for his appearance, whereupon Mr. Smith, the magistrate, remarked that under the present excited state of affairs, he did not think he would be justified in receiving bail from Nauvoo, as it was a matter of doubt whether property would not be rendered valueless there in a few days.

Knowing the party we had to deal with, we were not much surprised at this singular proceeding; we then remarked that both of us possessed property in farms out of Nauvoo in the country, and referred him to the county records. He then stated that such was the nature of the charge against Mr. Garn, that he believed he would not be justified in receiving any bail. We were thus confirmed in our opinion that the night's proceedings before, in relation to their desire to have us give bail, was a mere ruse to separate us. We were not permitted to speak with Garn, the real charge against whom was that he was traveling in Carthage or its neighborhood; what the fictitious one was, if I knew, I have since forgotten, as things of this kind were a daily occurrence.

After waiting the governor's pleasure for some time we had an audience; but such an audience!

He was surrounded by some of the vilest and most unprincipled men in creation; some of them had an appearance of respectability, and many of them lacked even that. Wilson, and I believe, William Law were there, Foster, Frank and Chauncey Higbee, Mr. Mar, a lawyer from Nauvoo, a mobocratic merchant from Warsaw, the aforesaid Jackson, a number of his associates, among whom was the governor's secretary; in all, some fifteen or twenty persons, most of whom were recreant to virtue, honor, integrity, and everything that is considered honorable among men.

I can well remember the feelings of disgust that I had in seeing the governor surrounded by such an infamous group, and on being introduced to men of so questionable a character; and had I been on private business, I should have turned to depart, and told the governor that if he thought proper to associate with such questionable characters, I should beg leave to be excused; but coming as we did on public business, we could not, of course, consult our private feelings.

We then stated to the governor that, in accordance with his request, General Smith had, in response to his call, sent us to him as a committee of conference; that we were acquainted with most of the circumstances that had transpired in and about Nauvoo lately, and were prepared to give him all information; that, moreover, we had in our possession testimony and affidavits confirmatory of what we should say, which had been forwarded to him by General Joseph Smith; that communications had been forwarded to his excellency by Messrs. Hunter, James, and others, some of which had not reached their destination, but of which we had duplicates with us. We then, in brief, related an outline of the difficulties, and the course we had pursued from the commencement of the troubles up to the present, and handing him the documents, respectfully submitted the whole.

During our conversation and explanations with the governor we were frequently rudely and impudently contradicted by the fellows he had around him, and of whom he seemed to take no notice.

He opened and read a number of the documents himself, and as he proceeded, he was frequently interrupted by "That's a lie!" "That's a G— d—ned lie!" "That's an infernal falsehood!" "That's a blasted lie!" etc.

These men evidently winced at an exposure of their acts, and thus vulgarly, impudently, and falsely repudiated them. One of their number, Mr. Mar, addressed himself several times to me while in conversation with the governor. I did not notice him until after frequent repetition of his insolence, when I informed him that "my business at that time was with Governor Ford", whereupon I continued my conversation with his excellency. During the conversation the governor expressed a desire that Joseph Smith, and all parties concerned in passing or executing the city law, in relation to the press, had better come to Carthage; that, however repugnant it might be to our feelings, he thought it would have a tendency to allay public excitement, and prove to the people what we professed, that we wished to be governed by law. We represented to him the course we had taken in relation to this matter, and our willingness to go before another magistrate other than the municipal court; the illegal refusal of our request by the constable; our dismissal by the municipal court, a legally constituted tribunal; our subsequent trial before Squire Wells at the instance by Judge Thomas, the circuit judge, and our dismissal by him; that we had fulfilled the law in every particular; that it was our enemies who were breaking the law, and, having murderous designs, were only making use of this as a pretext to get us into their power. The governor stated that the people viewed it differently, and that, notwithstanding our opinions, he would recommend that the people should be satisfied. We then remarked to him that, should Joseph Smith comply with his request, it would be extremely unsafe, in the present excited state of the country, to come without an armed force; that we had a sufficiency of men, and were competent to defend ourselves, but there might be danger of collision should our forces and that of our enemies be brought into such close proximity. He strenuously advised us not to bring any arms, and *pledged his faith as governor, and the faith of the state, that we should be protected, and that he would guarantee our perfect safety.*

We had at that time about five thousand men under arms, one thousand of whom would have been amply sufficient for our protection.

At the termination of our interview, and previous to our withdrawal, after a long conversation and the perusal of the documents which we had brought, the governor informed us that he would prepare a written communication for General Joseph Smith, which he desired us to wait for. We were kept waiting for this instrument some five or six hours.

NOTE

1. The Ford letter was reprinted in *Deseret News,* no. 33, 21 October 1857, p. 257 [MT].

COUNCIL CONVENED IN NAUVOO

A bout five o'clock in the afternoon we took our departure with not the most pleasant feelings. The associations of the governor, the spirit that he manifested to
compromise with these scoundrels, the length of time that
he had kept us waiting, and his general deportment,
together with the infernal spirit that we saw exhibited by
those whom he had admitted to his councils, made the
prospect anything but promising.

We returned on horseback, and arrived at Nauvoo, I
think, at about eight or nine o'clock at night accompanied
by Captain Yates in command of a company of mounted
men, who came for the purpose of escorting Joseph Smith
and the accused in case of their complying with the governor's request, and going to Carthage. We went directly to
Brother Joseph's, when Captain Yates delivered to him the
governor's communication. A council was called, consisting
of Joseph's brother Hyrum, Dr. Richards, Dr. Bernhisel,
myself, and one or two others.[1]

We then gave a detail of our interview with the governor. Brother Joseph was very much dissatisfied with the

governor's letter, and with his general deportment, and so were the council, and it became a serious question as to the course we should pursue. Various projects were discussed, but nothing definitely decided upon for some time.

In the interim two gentlemen arrived; one of them, if not both, sons of John C. Calhoun. They had come to Nauvoo, and were very anxious for an interview with Brother Joseph.

These gentlemen detained him for some time; and as our council was held in Dr. Bernhisel's room in the Mansion House, the doctor lay down; and as it was now between 2 and 3 o'clock in the morning, and I had had no rest on the previous night, I was fatigued, and thinking that Brother Joseph might not return, I left for home and rest.

Being very much fatigued, I slept soundly, and was somewhat surprised in the morning by Mrs. Thompson entering my room about 7 o'clock, and exclaiming in surprise, "What, you here? the brethren have crossed the river some time since."

"What brethren?" I asked.

"Brother Joseph, and Hyrum, and Brother Richards," she answered.

I immediately arose upon learning that they had crossed the river, and did not intend to go to Carthage. I called together a number of persons in whom I had confidence, and had the type, stereotype plates, and most of the valuable things removed from the printing office, believing that should the governor and his force come to Nauvoo, the first thing they would do would be to burn the printing office, for I know that they would be exasperated if Brother

Joseph went away. We had talked over these matters the night before, but nothing was decided upon. It was Brother Joseph's opinion that, should we leave for a time, public excitement, which was so intense, would be allayed; that it would throw on the governor the responsibility for keeping the peace; that in the event of an outrage, the onus would rest upon the governor, who was amply prepared with troops, and could command all the forces of the state to preserve order; and that the act of his own men would be an overwhelming proof of their seditious designs, not only to the governor, but to the world. He moreover thought that, in the east, where he intended to go, public opinion would be set right in relation to these matters, and its expression would partially influence the west, and that, after the first ebullition things would assume a shape that would justify his return.

I made arrangements for crossing the river, and Brother Elias Smith and Joseph Cain, who were both employed in the printing office with me, assisted all that lay in their power together with Brother Brower and several hands in the printing office. As we could not find out the exact whereabouts of Joseph and the brethren, I crossed the river in a boat furnished by Brother Cyrus H. Wheelock and Alfred Bell; and after the removal of the things of the printing office, Joseph Cain brought the account books to me, that we might make arrangements for their adjustment; and Brother Elias Smith, cousin to Brother Joseph, went to obtain money for the journey, and also to find out and report me the location of the brethren.

As Cyrus Wheelock was an active, enterprising man,

and in the event of not finding Brother Joseph I calculated to go to Upper Canada for the time being, and should need a companion, I said to Brother Cyrus H. Wheelock, "Can you go with me ten or fifteen hundred miles?"

He answered, "Yes."

"Can you start in half an hour?"

"Yes."

However I told him that he had better see his family, who lived over the river, and prepare a couple of horses and the necessary equippage for the journey; and that, if we did not find Brother Joseph before, we would start at nightfall.

A laughable incident occurred on the eve of my departure. After making all the preparations I could, previous to leaving Nauvoo, and having bid adieu to my family, I went to a house adjoining the river, owned by Brother Eddy. There I disguised myself so as not to be known, and so effectually was the transformation, that those who had come after me with a boat did not know me. I went down to the boat and sat in it. Brother Bell, thinking it was a stranger, watched my moves for some time very impatiently, and then said to Brother Wheelock, "I wish that old gentleman would go away; he has been pottering around the boat for some time, and I am afraid Elder Taylor will be coming." When he discovered his mistake, he was not a little amused.

I was conducted by Brother Bell to a house that was surrounded by timber on the opposite side of the river. There I spent several hours in a chamber with Brother Joseph Cain, adjusting my accounts; and I made arrangements for the stereotype plates of the *Book of Mormon,* and

Doctrine and Covenants, to be forwarded east, thinking to supply the company with subsistence money through the sale of these books in the east.

NOTE

1. See Letter file in Church Historian's Office, "Ford", 1844. Contents of this letter [are] sufficiently given in the conversation between Joseph Smith and Governor Ford in Carthage prison [B. H. Roberts's note; hereafter, all such identified as BHR].

Chapter 6

JOSEPH RETURNS

———

My horses were reported ready by Brother Wheelock, and funds on hand by Brother Elias Smith. In about half an hour I should have started, when Brother Elias Smith came to me with word that he had found the brethren; that they had concluded to go to Carthage, and wished me to return to Nauvoo and accompany them. I must confess that I felt a good deal disappointed at this news, but I immediately made preparations to go. Escorted by Brother Elias Smith, I and my party went to the neighborhood of Montrose, where we met Brother Joseph, Hyrum, Brother Richards and others. Dr. Bernhisel thinks that W. W. Phelps was not with Joseph and Hyrum in the morning, but that he met him, myself, and Joseph and Hyrum, Willard Richards, and Brother Calhoun, in the afternoon, near Montrose, returning to Nauvoo.

On meeting the brethren I learned that it was not Brother Joseph's desire to return, but that he came back by request of some of the brethren, and that it coincided more with Brother Hyrum's feelings than with those of Brother Joseph. In fact, after his return, Brother Hyrum expressed himself as perfectly satisfied with the course taken, and said that he felt much more at ease in his mind than he did before. On our return the calculation was to throw ourselves under the immediate protection of the governor, and to trust to his word and faith for our preservation.

A message was, I believe, sent to the governor that night, stating that we should come to Carthage in the morning, the party that came along with us to escort us back, in case we returned to Carthage, having returned.

It would seem from the following remarks of Governor Ford, that there was a design on foot, which was, that if we refused to go to Carthage at the governor's request, there should be an increased force called for by the governor, and that we should be destroyed by them. In accordance with this project, Captain Yates returned with his *posse,* accompanied by the constable who held the writ.

The following is the governor's remark in relation to this affair:

> The constable and his escort returned. The constable made no effort to arrest any of them, nor would he or the guard delay their departure one minute beyond the time, to see whether an arrest could be made. Upon their return they reported that they had been informed that the accused had fled, and could not be found. I immediately proposed to a council of officers to march into Nauvoo with the small force then under my command, but the officers were of the opinion that it was too small, and many of them insisted upon a further call of the militia. Upon reflection I was of the opinion that the officers were right in the esti-

mate of our force, and the project for immediate action was abandoned.

I was soon informed, however, of the conduct of constable and guard, and then I was perfectly satisfied that a most base fraud had been attempted; that, in fact, it was feared that the "Mormons" would submit, and thereby entitle themselves to the protection of the law. It was very apparent that many of the bustling active spirits were afraid that there would be no occasion for calling out an overwhelming militia force, for marching it into Nauvoo, for probable mutiny when there, and for the extermination of the "Mormon" race. It appeared that the constable and the escort were fully in the secret, and acted well their part to promote the conspiracy.[1]

In the morning Brother Joseph had an interview with the officers of the Legion, with the leading members of the city council, and with the principal men of the city. The officers were instructed to dismiss their men, but to have them in a state of readiness to be called upon in any emergency that might occur.

About half-past six o'clock the members of the city council, the marshal, Brothers Joseph and Hyrum, and a number of others started for Carthage, on horseback. We were instructed by Brother Joseph Smith not to take any arms, and we consequently left them behind. We called at the house of Brother Fellows on our way out. Brother Fellows lives about four miles from Carthage.

While at Brother Fellows' house, Captain Dunn, accompanied by Mr. Coolie, one of the governor's aid-de-camps, came up from Carthage en route for Nauvoo with a requisition from the governor for the state arms. We all returned to Nauvoo with them; the governor's request was complied with, and after taking some refreshments, we all returned to proceed to Carthage. We arrived there late in the night. A great deal of excitement prevailed on and after our arrival. The governor had received into his company all of the companies that had been in the mob; these fellows were riotous and disorderly, hallooing, yelling, and whooping about the streets like Indians, many of them intoxicated; the whole presented a scene of rowdyism and low-bred ruffianism only found among mobocrats and desperadoes, and entirely revolting to the best feelings of humanity. The governor made a speech to them to the effect that he would show Joseph and Hyrum Smith to them in the morning.

About here the companies with the governor were drawn up into line, and General Deming, I think, took Joseph by the arm and Hyrum (Arnold says that Joseph took the governor's arm), and as he passed through between the ranks, the governor leading in front, very politely introduced them as General Joseph Smith and General Hyrum Smith.[2]

All were orderly and courteous except one company of mobocrats—the Carthage Greys—who seemed to find fault on account of too much honor being paid to the Mormons. There was afterward a row between the companies, and they came pretty near having a fight; the more orderly not feeling disposed to endorse or submit to the rowdyism of the mobocrats. The result was that General Deming, who was very much of a gentleman, ordered the Carthage Greys, a company under the command of Captain [Robert F.]

Smith, a magistrate in Carthage, and a most violent mobo-crat, under arrest. This matter, however, was shortly after-ward adjusted, and the difficulty settled between them.

The mayor, aldermen, councilors, as well as the marshal of the city of Nauvoo, together with some persons who had assisted the marshal in removing the press in Nauvoo, appeared before Justice Smith, the aforesaid captain and mobocrat, to again answer the charge of destroying the press; but as there was so much excitement, and as the man was an unprincipled villain before whom we were to have our hearing, we thought it most prudent to give bail, and consequently became security for each other in $500 bonds each, to appear before the county court at its next session. We had engaged as counsel a lawyer by the name of Wood, of Burlington, Iowa; and Reed, I think, of Madison, Iowa. After some little discussion the bonds were signed, and we were all dismissed.

NOTES

1. Ford's *History of Illinois,* p. 333 [JT].

2. The *Deseret News* gives the following account of Joseph and Hyrum Smith's passing through the troops at Carthage:—

Carthage, June 25th, 1844.

Quarter-past 9. The governor came and invited Joseph to walk with him through the troops. Joseph solicited a few moments' private conversation with him, which the governor refused.

While refusing, the governor looked down at his shoes, as though he was ashamed. They then walked through the crowd, with Brigadier-General Miner, R. Deming, and Dr. Richards, to General Deming's quarters. The people appeared quiet until a company of Carthage Greys flocked round the doors of General Deming in an uproarious manner, of which notice was sent to the governor. In the meantime the governor had ordered the McDonough troops to be drawn up in line, for Joseph and Hyrum to pass in front of them, they having requested that they might have a clear view of the General Smiths. *Joseph had a conversation with the governor for about ten minutes, when he again pledged the faith of the state that he and his friends should be protected from violence.*

Robinson, the postmaster, said, on report of martial law being proclaimed in Nauvoo, he had stopped the mail, and notified the postmaster-general of the state of things in Hancock county.

From the general's quarters Joseph and Hyrum went in front of the lines in a hollow square of a company of Carthage Greys. At seven minutes before ten they arrived in front of the lines, and passed before the whole, Joseph being on the right of General Deming and Hyrum on his left, Elders Richards, Taylor, and Phelps following. Joseph and Hyrum were introduced by Governor Ford about twenty times along the line as General Joseph Smith and General Hyrum Smith, the governor walking in front on the left. The Carthage Greys refused to receive them by that introduction, and some of the officers threw up their hats, drew their swords, and said they would introduce themselves to the damned "Mormons" in a different style. The governor mildly entreated them not to act so rudely, but their excitement increased; the governor, however, succeeded in pacifying them by making a speech, and promising them that they should have "full satisfaction." General Smith and party returned to their lodgings at five minutes past 10. *Deseret News,* no. 35, 4 Nov. 1857, p. 274 [JT].

Chapter 7

IMPRISONED FOR "TREASON"

———

Almost immediately after our dismissal, two men—
Augustine Spencer and Norton—two worthless fellows,
whose words would not have been taken for five cents,
and the first of whom had a short time previously been
before the mayor in Nauvoo for maltreating a lame brother,
made affidavits that Joseph and Hyrum Smith were guilty
of treason, and a writ was accordingly issued for their arrest,
and the Constable Bettisworth, a rough, unprincipled man,
wished immediately to hurry them away to prison without
any hearing. His rude, uncouth manner in the administra-
tion of what he considered the duties of his office made him
exceedingly repulsive to us all. But, independent of these
acts, the proceedings in this case were altogether illegal.
Providing the court was sincere, which it was not, and providing these men's oaths were true, and that Joseph and
Hyrum were guilty of treason, still the whole course was
illegal.

The magistrate made out a mittimus, and committed
them to prison without a hearing, which he had no right
legally to do. The statute of Illinois expressly provides that

"all men shall have a hearing before a magistrate before they shall be committed to prison"; and Mr. Robert F. Smith, the magistrate, had made out a mittimus committing them to prison contrary to law without such hearing. As I was informed of this illegal proceeding, I went immediately to the governor and informed him of it. Whether he was apprised of it before or not, I do not know; but my opinion is that he was.

I represented to him the characters of the parties who had made oath, the outrageous nature of the charge, the indignity offered to men in the position which they occupied, and declared to him that he knew very well it was a vexatious proceeding, and that the accused were not guilty of any such crime. The governor replied, he was very sorry that the thing had occurred; that he did not believe the charges, but that he thought the best thing to be done was to let the law take its course. I then reminded him that we had come out there at his instance, not to satisfy the law, which we had done before, but the prejudices of the people, in relation to the affair of the press; that at his instance we had given bonds, which we could not by law be required to do to satisfy the people, and that it was asking too much to require gentlemen in their position in life to suffer the degradation of being immured in a jail at the instance of such worthless scoundrels as those who had made this affidavit. The governor replied that it was an unpleasant affair, and looked very hard; but that it was a matter over which he had no control, as it belonged to the judiciary; that he, as the executive, could not interfere with their proceedings, and that he had no doubt but that they would immediately be dismissed. I told him that we had looked to him for protection from such insults, and that I thought we had a right to do so from the solemn promises which he had made to me and to Dr. Bernhisel in relation to our coming without guard or arms; that we had relied upon his faith, and had a right to expect him to fulfill his engagements after we had placed ourselves implicitly under his care, and complied with all his requests, although extra-judicial.

He replied that he would detail a guard, if we required it, and see us protected, but that he could not interfere with the judiciary. I expressed my dissatisfaction at the course taken, and told him that if we were to be subject to mob rule, and to be dragged, contrary to law, into prison at the instance of every infernal scoundrel whose oaths could be bought for a dram of whiskey, his protection availed very little, and we had miscalculated his promises.

Seeing there was no prospect of redress from the governor, I returned to the room and found the Constable Bettisworth very urgent to hurry Brothers Joseph and Hyrum to prison, whilst the brethren were remonstrating with him. At the same time a great rabble was gathered in the streets and around the door, and from the rowdyism manifested I was afraid there was a design to murder the prisoners on the way to the jail.

Without conferring with any person, my next feelings were to procure a guard, and, seeing a man habited as a soldier in the room, I went to him and said, "I am afraid there is a design against the lives of the Messrs. Smith; will you go immediately and bring your captain; and, if not convenient,

any other captain of a company, and I will pay you well for
your trouble?" He said he would, and departed forthwith,
and soon returned with his captain, whose name I have forgotten, and introduced him to me. I told him of my fears,
and requested him immediately to fetch his company.

He departed forthwith, and arrived at the door with
them just at the time when the constable was hurrying the
brethren downstairs. A number of the brethren went along,
together with one or two strangers; and all of us safely
lodged in prison, remained there during the night.

Chapter 8

JOSEPH'S INTERVIEW
WITH GOVERNOR FORD

——

At the request of Joseph Smith for an interview with the governor, he came the next morning, Thursday, June 26th, at half past 9 o'clock, accompanied by Colonel Thomas Geddes, when a lengthy conversation was entered into in relation to the existing difficulties; and after some preliminary remarks, at the governor's request, Brother Joseph gave him a general outline of the state of affairs in relation to our difficulties, the excited state of the country, the tumultuous mobocratic movements of our enemies, the precautionary measures used by himself (Joseph Smith), the acts of the city council, the destruction of the press, and the moves of the mob and ourselves up to that time.

The following report is, I believe, substantially correct:

Governor—"General Smith: I believe you have given me a general outline of the difficulties that have existed in the country in the documents forwarded to me by Dr. Bernhisel and Mr. Taylor; but, unfortunately, there seems to be a great discrepancy between your statements and those of your enemies. It is true that you are substantiated by evidence and affidavit, but for such an extraordinary excitement as that which is now in the country there must be some cause, and I attribute the last outbreak to the destruction of the *Expositor,* and to your refusal to comply with the writ issued by Esquire Morrison. The press in the United States is looked upon as the great bulwark of American freedom, and its destruction in Nauvoo was represented and looked upon as a high-handed measure, and manifests to the people a disposition on your part to suppress the liberty of speech and of the press. This, with your refusal to comply with the requisition of a writ, I conceive to be the principal cause of this difficulty; and you are moreover represented to me as turbulent, and defiant of the laws and institutions of your country."

General Smith—"Governor Ford: you, sir, as governor of this state, are aware of the persecutions that I have endured. You know well that our course has been peaceable and law-abiding for I have furnished this state ever since our settlement here with sufficient evidence of my pacific intentions, and those of the people with whom I am associated, by the endurance of every conceivable indignity and lawless outrage perpetrated upon me and upon this people since our settlement here; and you yourself know that I have kept you well posted in relation to all matters associated with the late difficulties. If you have not got some of my communication, it has not been my fault.

"Agreeably to your orders, I assembled the Nauvoo Legion for the protection of Nauvoo and the surrounding country against an armed band of marauders; and ever since they have been mustered, I have almost daily communicated with you in regard to all the leading events that have transpired; and whether in the capacity of mayor of the city, or lieutenant-general of the Nauvoo Legion, I have striven, according to the best of my judgment to preserve the peace and to administer even-handed justice; but my motives are impugned, my acts are misconstrued, and I am grossly and wickedly misrepresented. I suppose I am indebted for my incarceration to the oath of a worthless man who was arraigned before me and fined for abusing and maltreating his lame, helpless brother. That I should be charged by you, sir, who know better, of acting contrary to law, is to me a matter of surprise. Was it the 'Mormons' or our enemies who first commenced these difficulties? You know well it was not us; and when this turbulent, outrageous people commenced their insurrectionary movements I made you acquainted with them officially, and asked your advice, and have followed strictly your counsel in every particular. Who ordered out the Nauvoo Legion?—I did, under your direction. For what purpose?—To suppress the insurrectionary movements. It was at your instance, sir, that I issued a proclamation calling upon the Nauvoo Legion to be in readiness at a moment's warning to guard against the incursions of mobs, and gave an order to Jonathan Dunham, acting major-general, to that effect.

"Am I, then, to be charged for the acts of others? and because lawlessness and mobocracy abound, am I, when carrying out your instructions, to be charged with not abiding law? Why is it that I must be made accountable for other men's acts? If there is trouble in the country, neither I nor my people made it; and all that we have ever done, after much endurance on our part, is to maintain and uphold the Constitution and institutions of our country, and to protect an injured, innocent, and persecuted people against misrule and mob violence.

"Concerning the destruction of the press to which you refer, men may differ somewhat in their opinions about it; but can it be supposed that after all the indignities to which they have been subjected outside, that people would suffer a set of worthless vagabonds to come into their city, and, right under their own eyes and protection, vilify and calumniate not only themselves, but the character of their wives and daughters, as was impudently and unblushingly done in that infamous and filthy sheet?

"There is not a city in the United States that would have suffered such an indignity for twenty-four hours. Our whole people were indignant, and loudly called upon our city authorities for a redress of their grievances, which, if not attended to, they themselves would have taken into their own hands, and have summarily punished the audacious wretches as they deserved. The principle of equal rights that has been instilled into our bosoms from our cradles as American citizens forbids us submitting to every foul indignity, and succumbing and pandering to wretches so infamous as these. But, independent of this, the course that we pursued we considered to be strictly legal; for, notwithstanding the result, we were anxious to be governed strictly by law, and therefore we convened the city council; and being desirous in our deliberations to abide by law, we summoned legal counsel to be present on the occasion.

Upon investigating the matter, we found that our city charter gave us power to remove all nuisances. Furthermore, after consulting Blackstone[1] upon what might be considered a nuisance, it appeared that that distinguished lawyer, who is considered authority, I believe, in all courts, states among other things that 'a libelous and filthy press may be considered a nuisance, and abated as such.'[2] Here, then, one of the most eminent English barristers, whose works are considered standard with us, declares that a libelous and filthy press may be considered a nuisance; and our own charter, given us by the legislature of this state, gives us the power to remove nuisances; and by ordering that press to be abated as a nuisance, we conceived that we were acting strictly in accordance with law. We made that order in our corporate capacity, and the city marshal carried it out. It is possible there may have been some better way, but I must confess that I could not see it.

"In relation to the writ served upon us, we were willing to abide the consequences of our own acts, but were unwilling, in answering a writ of that kind, to submit to illegal exactions, sought to be imposed upon under the pretense of law, when we knew they were in open violation of it. When that document was presented to me by Mr. Bettisworth, I offered, in the presence of more than twenty persons, to go to any other magistrate, either in our city, in Appanoose, or any other place where we should be safe, but we all refused to put ourselves into the power of a mob. What right had that constable to refuse our request? He had none according to law; for you know, Governor Ford, that the statute law in Illinois is, that the parties served with the writ 'shall go before him who issued it, or *some other justice of the peace.*' Why, then, should we be dragged to Carthage, where the law does not compel us to go? Does not this look like many others of our persecutions with which you are acquainted? and have we not a right to expect foul play? This very act was a breach of law on his part, an assumption of power that did not belong to him, and an attempt, at least, to deprive us of our legal and constitutional rights and privileges. What could we do, under the circumstances, different from what we did do? We sued for, and obtained a writ of *habeas corpus* from the municipal court, by which we were delivered from the hands of Constable Bettisworth, and brought before and acquitted by the municipal court. After our acquittal, in a conversation with Judge Thomas, although he considered the acts of the party illegal, he advised that, to satisfy the people, we had better go before another magistrate who was not in our church. In accordance with his advice, we went before Esquire Wells, with whom you are well acquainted; both parties were present, witnesses were called on both sides, the case was fully investigated, and we were again dismissed. And what is this pretended desire to enforce law, and wherefore are these lying, base rumors put into circulation but to seek, through mob influence, under pretense of law, to make us submit to requisitions which are contrary to law and subversive of every principle of justice? And when you, sir, required us to come out here, we came, not because it was legal, but because you required it of us, and we were desirous of showing to you, and to all men, that we shrunk not from the most rigid investigation of our acts. We certainly did expect other treatment than to be immured in a jail at the instance of these men, and I think, from your plighted faith, we had a right so to expect, after disbanding our own forces, and putting ourselves entirely in your hands. And now, after having fulfilled my part, sir, as a man and an American citizen, I call up you, Governor Ford, to deliver us from this place, and rescue us from this outrage that is sought to be practiced upon us by a set of infamous scoundrels."

Governor Ford—"But you have placed men under arrest, detained men as prisoners, and given passes to others, some of which I have seen."

John P. Greene, City Marshal—"Perhaps I can explain. Since these difficulties have commenced, you are aware that we have been placed under very peculiar circumstances; our city has been placed under a very rigid police guard; in addition to this, frequent guards have been placed outside the city to prevent any sudden surprise, and those guards have questioned suspected or suspicious persons as to their business. To strangers, in some instances, passes have been given to prevent difficulty in passing those guards; it is some of these passes that you have seen. No person, sir, has been imprisoned without a legal cause in our city."

Governor [Ford]—"Why did you not give a more speedy answer to the *posse* that I sent out?"

General Smith—"We had matters of importance to consult upon; your letter showed anything but an amiable spirit. We have suffered immensely in Missouri from mobs, in loss of property, imprisonment, and otherwise. It took some time for us to weigh duly these matters; we could not decide upon matters of such importance immediately, and your *posse* were too hasty in returning; we were consulting for a large people, and vast interests were at stake. We had been outrageously imposed upon, and knew not how far we could trust anyone, besides, a question necessarily arose, how shall we come? Your request was that we should come unarmed. It became a matter of serious importance to decide how far promises could be trusted, and how far we were safe from mob violence."

Colonel Geddes—"It certainly did look from all I have heard, from the general spirit of violence and mobocracy that here prevails, that it was not safe for you to come unprotected."[3]

Governor Ford—"I think that sufficient time was not allowed by the *posse* for you to consult and get ready. They were too hasty; but I suppose they found themselves bound by their orders. I think, too, there is a great deal of truth in what you say, and your reasoning is plausible, but I must beg leave to differ from you in relation to the acts of the city council. That council, in my opinion, had no right to act in a legislative capacity and in that of the judiciary. They should have passed a law in relation to the matter, and then the municipal court, upon complaint, could have removed it [i.e., the *Expositor* press]; but for the city council to take upon themselves the law-making and the execution of the law, is, in my opinion, wrong; besides, these men ought to have had a hearing before their property was destroyed; to destroy it without was an infringement on their rights; besides, it is so contrary to the feelings of American people to interfere with the press. And furthermore, I cannot but think that it would have been more judicious for you to have gone with Mr. Bettisworth to Carthage, notwithstanding the law did not require it. Concerning your being in jail, I am sorry for that; I wish it had been otherwise. I hope you will soon be released, but I can not interfere."

Joseph Smith—"Governor Ford, allow me, sir, to bring one thing to your mind that you seem to have overlooked. You state that you think it would have been better for us to have submitted to the requisition of Constable Bettisworth, and to have gone to Carthage. Do you not know, sir, that that writ was served at the instance of an anti-'Mormon' mob, who had passed resolutions and published them to the effect that they would exterminate the 'Mormon' leaders? And are you not informed that Captain Anderson was not only threatened, but had a gun fired at his boat by this said mob in Warsaw when coming up to Nauvoo, and that this very thing was made use of as a means to get us into their hands; and we could not, without taking an armed force with us, go there without, according to their published declarations, going into the jaws of death? To have taken a force with us, would only have fanned the excitement, and they would have stated that we wanted to use intimidation; therefore, we thought it the most judicious to avail ourselves of the protection of law."

Governor Ford—"I see, I see."

Joseph Smith—"Furthermore, in relation to the press, you say that you differ from me in opinion. Be it so, the thing, after all, is only a legal difficulty, and the courts, I should judge, are competent to decide on that matter. If our act was illegal, we are willing to meet it and although I can not see the distinction that you draw about the acts of the city council, and what difference it could have made in point of fact, law, or justice between the city council's acting together or separate, or how much more legal it would have been for the municipal court, who were a part of the city council, to act separately instead of with the councilors, yet, if it is deemed that we did a wrong in destroying that press, we refuse not to pay for it; we are desirous to fulfill the law in every particular, and are responsible for our acts. You say that the parties ought to have had a hearing. Had it been a civil suit, this, of course, would have been proper; but there was a flagrant violation of every principle of right—a nuisance; and it was abated on the same principle that any nuisance, stench, or putrefied carcass would have been removed. Our first step, therefore, was to stop the foul, noisome, filthy sheet, and then the next in our opinion would have been to have prosecuted the man for a breach of public decency. And, furthermore, again let me say, Governor Ford, I shall look to you for our protection. I believe you are talking of going to Nauvoo; if you go, sir, I wish to go along. I refuse not to answer any law, but I do not consider myself safe here."

Governor—"I am in hopes that you will be acquitted, and if I go I will certainly take you along. I do not, however, apprehend danger. I think you are perfectly safe either here or anywhere else. I can not, however, interfere with the law. I am placed in peculiar circumstances, and seem to be blamed by all parties."

Joseph Smith—"Governor Ford, I ask nothing but what is legal; I have a right to expect protection, at least from you; for, independent of law, you have pledged your faith and that of the state for my protection, and I wish to go to Nauvoo."

Governor—"And you shall have protection, General Smith. I did not make this promise without consulting my officers, who all pledged their honor to its fulfillment. I do not know that I shall go tomorrow to Nauvoo, but if I do I will take you along."

At a quarter past ten o'clock the governor left.

NOTES

1. Sir William Blackstone, professor, judge, and author, appears to have had a virtually singular influence on the development of early American law. As there were few purely American legal precedents or writings during the nation's infancy, his four-volume *Commentaries on the Laws of England* (Oxford, 1769) served as the standard of American Lawyers well into the nineteenth century. As of 1860, nearly as many copies of those volumes had been sold in the U.S. as in England, despite the large disparity in population. Hence, that his commentaries were consulted during the City Council's deliberations at this time was essential [MT].

2. The author referred to (Blackstone) says: "A fourth species of remedy by the mere act of the party injured, is the abatement, or removal of nuisances." On this the following commentary is made in note 6. "So it seems that a *libelous print, or paper* [not the printing press on which they may have been printed] affecting a private individual may be destroyed; or, which is the better course, taken and delivered to a magistrate" (See Chitty's *Blackstone,* bk. ii, chs. i, iv, note 6). The destruction of libelous *"prints and papers"* can scarcely be held to sustain the action of destroying a *"printing press"* [BHR].

The reader should note the Chitty's version of Blackstone was not published until 1848. Hence, they had not access to notes (prepared and included by Chitty) referenced by B. H. Roberts in the *History.* Other versions, like Christian's 1807 version of Blackstone's Commentaries, don't contain Chitty's remarks (and any inferences drawn therefrom) [MT].

3. Notwithstanding this sympathetic allusion by Colonel Geddes upon the situation, it is stated by Gregg that Geddes was really unfriendly to the Prophet and had no sympathy with him and the injustice which had been done him in his arrest and imprisonment, for after leaving the prison and carrying on a conversation with Governor Ford, he represents the governor as saying to him: "O, it's all nonsense; you will have to drive these Mormons out yet!" Then Geddes said to the governor: "If we undertake that governor, when the proper time comes, will you interfere?" "No, I will not," said the governor, after a pause adding, *"until you are through"* (Gregg's *History of Hancock County,* p. 372) [BHR].

Chapter 9

A POOR WAYFARING MAN

———

At about half past twelve o'clock Mr. Reed, one of Joseph's counsel, came in, apparently much elated; he stated that, upon an examination of the law, he found that the magistrate had transcended his jurisdiction, and that, having committed them without an examination, his jurisdiction ended; that he had him upon a pinhook; that he ought to have examined them before he committed them, and that, having violated the law in this particular, he had no farther power over them; for, once committed, they were out of his jurisdiction, as the power of the magistrate extended no farther than their committal, and that now they could not be brought out except at the regular session of the circuit court, or by a writ of *habeas corpus;* but that if Justice Smith would consent to go to Nauvoo for trial, he would compromise matters with him, and overlook this matter.

Mr. Reed farther stated, that the anti-"Mormons," or mob had concocted a scheme to get a writ from Missouri, with a demand upon Governor Ford for the arrest of Joseph Smith and his conveyance to Missouri, and that a man by the name of Wilson had returned from Missouri the night before the burning of the press for this purpose.

At half past two o'clock Constable Bettisworth came to the jail with a man named Simpson, professing to have some order, but he would not send up his name, and the guard would not let him pass. Dr. Bernhisel and Brother Wasson went to inform the governor and council of this. At about twenty minutes to three Dr. Bernhisel returned, and stated that he thought the governor was doing all he could. At about ten minutes to three Hirum Kimball appeared with news from Nauvoo.

Soon after Constable Bettisworth came with an order from Esquire Smith to convey the prisoners to the court-house for trial. He was informed that the process was illegal, that they had been placed there contrary to law, and that they refused to come unless by legal process. I was informed that Justice [Robert F.] Smith (who was also Captain of the Carthage Greys) went to the governor and informed him of the matter, and that the governor replied: "You have your forces, and of course can use them." The constable certainly did return, accompanied by a guard of armed men, and by force, and under protest, hurried the prisoners to the court.

About four o'clock the case was called by Captain Robert F. Smith, J.P. The counsel for the prisoners called for subpoenas to bring witnesses. At twenty-five minutes past four he took a copy of the order to bring the prisoners from jail to trial, and afterwards he took names of witnesses.

Counsel present for the state: Higbee, Skinner, Sharpe,

Emmons, and Morrison. Twenty-five minutes to five the writ was returned as served, June 25th.

Many remarks were made at the court that I paid but little attention to, as I considered the whole thing illegal and a complete burlesque. Wood objected to the proceedings *in toto,* in consequent of its illegality, showing that the prisoners were not only illegally committed, but that, being once committed, the magistrate had no farther power over them; but as it was the same magistrate before whom he was pleading who imprisoned them contrary to law, and the same who, as a captain, forced them from jail, his arguments availed but little. He then urged that the prisoners be remanded until witnesses could be had, and applied for a continuance for that purpose. Skinner suggested until twelve o'clock next day. Wood again demanded until witnesses could be obtained; that the court meet at a specified time, and that, if witnesses were not present, again adjourn, without calling the prisoners. After various remarks from Reed, Skinner, and others, the court stated, that the writ was served yesterday, and that it will give until tomorrow at twelve m. to get witnesses.

We then returned to jail. Immediately after our return Dr. Bernhisel went to the governor, and obtained from him an order for us to occupy a large, open room containing a bedstead. I rather think that the same room had been appropriated to the use of debtors; at any rate, there was free access to the jailer's house, and no bars or locks except such as might be on the outside door of the jail. The jailer, Mr. George W. Steghall, and his wife, manifested a disposition to make us as comfortable as they could; we ate at their table, which was well provided, and, of course, paid for it.

I do not remember the names of all who were with us that night and the next morning in jail, for several went and came; among those that we considered stationary were Stephen Markham, John S. Fullmer, Captain Dan Jones, Dr. Willard Richards, and myself. Dr. Bernhisel says that he was there from Wednesday in the afternoon until eleven o'clock next day. We were, however, visited by numerous friends, among whom were Uncle John Smith, Hirum Kimball, Cyrus H. Wheelock, besides lawyers, as counsel. There was also a great variety of conversation, which was rather desultory than otherwise, and referred to circumstances that had transpired, our former and present grievances, the spirit of the troops around us, and the disposition of the governor; the devising for legal and other plans for deliverance; the nature of testimony required; the gathering of proper witnesses; and a variety of other topics, including our religious hopes, etc.

During one of these conversations Dr. Richards remarked: "Brother Joseph, if it is necessary that you die in this matter, and if they will take me in your stead, I will suffer for you." At another time, when conversing about deliverance, I said, "Brother Joseph, if you will permit it, and say the word, I will have you out of this prison in five hours, if the jail has to come down to do it." My idea was to go to Nauvoo, and collect a force sufficient, as I considered the whole concern a legal farce, and a flagrant outrage upon our liberty and rights. Brother Joseph refused.

Elder Cyrus H. Wheelock came in to see us, and when

he was about leaving drew a small pistol, a six-shooter, from his pocket, remarking at the same time, "Would any of you like to have this?" Brother Joseph immediately replied, "Yes, give it to me," whereupon he took the pistol, and put it in his pantaloons pocket. The pistol was a six-shooting revolver, of Allen's Patent; it belonged to me, and was one that I furnished to Brother Wheelock when he talked of going with me to the east, previous to our coming to Carthage. I have it now in my possession. Brother Wheelock went out on some errand, and was not suffered to return. The report of the governor having gone to Nauvoo without taking the prisoners along with him caused very unpleasant feelings, as we were apprised that we were left to the tender mercies of the Carthage Greys, a company strictly mobocratic, and whom we knew to be our most deadly enemies; and their Captain, Esquire [Robert F.] Smith, was a most unprincipled villain. Besides this, all the mob forces, comprising the governor's troops, were dismissed, with the exception of one or two companies, which the governor took with him to Nauvoo. The great part of the mob was liberated, the remainder was our guard.

We looked upon it not only as a breach of faith on the part of the governor, but also as an indication of a desire to insult us, if nothing more, by leaving us in the proximity of such men. The prevention of Wheelock's return was among the first of their hostile movements.

Colonel Markham went out, and he was also prevented from returning. He was very angry at this, but the mob paid no attention to him; they drove him out of town at the point of the bayonet, and threatened to shoot him if he returned. He went, I am informed, to Nauvoo for the purpose of raising a company of men for our protection. Brother Fullmer went to Nauvoo after witnesses: it is my opinion that Brother Wheelock did also.

Sometime after dinner we sent for some wine. It has been reported by some that this was taken as a sacrament. It was no such thing; our spirits were generally dull and heavy, and it was sent for to revive us. I think it was Captain Jones who went after it, but they would not suffer him to return. I believe we all drank of the wine, and gave some to one or two of the prison guards. We all of us felt unusually dull and languid, with a remarkable depression of spirits. In consonance with those feelings I sang the following song, that had lately been introduced into Nauvoo, entitled, "A Poor Wayfaring Man of Grief," etc.[1]

The song is pathetic, and the tune quite plaintive, and was very much in accordance with our feelings at the time for our spirits were all depressed, dull and gloomy and surcharged with indefinite ominous forebodings. After a lapse of some time, Brother Hyrum requested me again to sing that song. I replied, "Brother Hyrum, I do not feel like singing;" when he remarked, "Oh! never mind, commence singing, and you will get the spirit of it." At his request I did so.

NOTE

1. The text of the hymn follows [MT]:

A Poor Wayfaring Man

1

A poor wayfaring man of grief
Hath often cross'd me on my way;
Who sued so humbly for relief,
That I could never answer, Nay.

2

I had not power to ask his name,
Whither to he went, or whence he came;
Yet there was something in his eye
That won my love, I knew not why.

3

Once, when my scanty meal was spread,
He enter'd—not a word he spake!
Just perishing for want of bread;
I gave him all: he bless'd it brake,

4

And ate, but gave me part again;
Mine was an angel's portion then,
For while I fed with eager haste,
The crust was manna to my taste.

5

I spied him where a fountain burst
Clear from the rock—his strength was gone—
The heedless water mock'd his thirst,
He heard it, saw it hurrying on.

6

I ran and rais'd the suff'rer up,
Thrice from the stream he drain'd my cup,
Dipp'd, and return'd it running o'er;
I drank, and never thirsted more.

7

'Twas night, the floods were out, it blew
A winter hurricane aloof;

I heard his voice abroad, and flew
To bid him welcome to my roof.

8

I warm'd, I cloth'd, I cheer'd my guest,
I laid him on my couch to rest;
Then made the earth my bed, and seem'd
In Eden's garden, while I dream'd.

9

Stripp'd, wounded, beaten nigh to death,
I found him by the highway side;
I rous'd his pulse, brought back his breath,
Reviv'd his spirit, and supplied

10

Wine, oil, refreshment—he was heal'd;
I had myself a wound conceal'd:
But from that hour forgot the smart,
And peace bound up my broken heart.

11

In prison I saw him next—condemn'd
To meet a traitor's doom at morn;
The tide of lying tongues I stemm'd,
And honour'd him mid shame and scorn.

12

My friendship's utmost zeal to try,
He asked if I for him would die;
The flesh was weak, my blood ran chill;
But my free spirit cried, "I will."

13

Then in a moment to my view,
The stranger started from disguise;
The tokens in his hands I knew,
The Saviour stood before mine eyes.

14

He spake—and my poor name he named—
"Of me thou hast not been asham'd;
These deeds shall thy memorial be;
Fear not, thou didst them unto me."

Chapter 10

THE DEADLY DEED

———

Soon afterwards I was sitting at one of the front windows of the jail, when I saw a number of men, with painted faces, coming round the corner of the jail, and aiming towards the stairs. The other brethren had seen the same, for, as I went to the door, I found Brother Hyrum Smith and Dr. Richards already leaning against it. They both pressed against the door with their shoulders to prevent its being opened, as the lock and latch were comparatively useless. While in this position, the mob, who had come upstairs, and tried to open the door, probably thought it was locked, and fired a ball through the keyhole; at this Dr. Richards and Brother Hyrum leaped back from the door, with their faces towards it; almost instantly another ball passed through the panel of the door, and struck Brother Hyrum on the left side of the nose, entering his face and head. At the same instant, another ball from the outside entered his back, passing through his body and striking his watch. The ball came from the back, through the jail window, opposite the door, and must, from its range, have been fired from the Carthage Greys, who were placed there ostensibly for our protection, as the balls from the firearms, shot close by the jail, would have entered the ceiling, we being in the second story, and there never was a time after that when Hyrum could have received the latter wound. Immediately, when the ball struck him, he fell flat on his back, crying as he fell, "I am a dead man!" He never moved afterwards.

I shall never forget the feeling of deep sympathy and regard manifested in the countenance of Brother Joseph as he drew nigh to Hyrum, and, leaning over him exclaimed, "Oh! my poor, dear brother Hyrum!" He, however, instantly arose, and with a firm, quick step, and a determined expression of countenance, approached the door, and pulling the six-shooter left by Brother Wheelock from his pocket, opened the door slightly and snapped the pistol six successive times; only three of the barrels, however, were discharged. I afterwards understood that two or three were wounded by these discharges, two of whom, I am informed, died. I had in my hands a large, strong hickory stick brought there by Brother Markham, and left by him, which I had seized as soon as I saw the mob approach; and while Brother Joseph was firing the pistol, I stood close behind him. As soon as he had discharged it he stepped back, and I immediately took his place next to the door, while he occupied the one I had done while he was shooting. Brother Richards, at this time, had a knotty walking-stick in his hands belonging to me, and stood next to Brother Joseph, a little farther from the door, in an oblique direction, apparently to avoid the rake of the fire from the door. The firing of Brother Joseph made our assailants pause for a moment;

very soon after, however, they pushed the door some distance open, and protruded and discharged their guns into the room, when I parried them off with my stick, giving another direction to the balls.

It certainly was a terrible scene: streams of fire as thick as my arm passed by me as these men fired, and, unarmed as we were, it looked like certain death. I remember feeling as though my time had come, but I do not know when, in any critical position, I was more calm, unruffled, and energetic, and acted with more promptness and decision. It certainly was far from pleasant to be so near the muzzles of those firearms as they belched forth their liquid flame and deadly balls. While I was engaged in parrying the guns, Brother Joseph said, "That's right, Brother Taylor, parry them off as well as you can." These were the last words I ever heard him speak on earth.

Every moment the crowd at the door became more dense, as they were unquestionably pressed on by those in the rear ascending the stairs, until the whole entrance at the door was literally crowded with muskets and rifles, which, with the swearing, shouting, and demoniacal expressions of those outside the door and on the stairs, and the firing of guns, mingled with their horrid oaths and execrations, made it look like pandemonium let loose, and was, indeed, a fit representation of the horrid deed in which they were engaged.

After parrying the guns for some time, which now protruded thicker and farther into the room, and seeing no hope of escape or protection there, as we were now unarmed, it occurred to me that we might have some friends outside, and that there might be some chance of escape in that direction, but here there seemed to be none. As I expected them every moment to rush into the room— nothing but extreme cowardice having kept them out—as the tumult and pressure increased, without any other hope, I made a spring for the window which was right in front of the jail door, where the mob was standing, and also exposed to the fire of the Carthage Greys, who were stationed some ten or twelve rods off. The weather was hot, we all of us had our coats off, and the window was raised to admit air. As I reached the window, and was on the point of leaping out, I was struck by a ball from the door about midway of my thigh, which struck the bone, and flattened out almost to the size of a quarter of a dollar, and then passed on through the fleshy part to within about half an inch of the outside. I think some prominent nerve must have been severed or injured for, as soon as the ball struck me, I fell like a bird when shot, or an ox when struck by a butcher, and lost entirely and instantaneously all power of action or locomotion. I fell upon the windowsill and cried out, "I am shot!" Not possessing any power to move, I felt myself falling outside of the window, but immediately I fell inside, from some, at that time, unknown cause. When I struck the floor my animation seemed restored, as I have seen it sometimes in squirrels and birds after being shot. As soon as I felt the power of motion I crawled under the bed, which was in a corner of the room, not far from the window where I received my wound. While on the way and under the bed I was wounded in three other places; one ball entered a little below the left knee, and never was extracted; another entered the forepart of my left arm, a little above the wrist, and, passing down by the joint, lodged in the fleshy part of my hand, about midway, a little above the upper joint of my little finger; another struck me on the fleshy part of my left hip, and tore away the flesh as large as my hand, dashing the mangled fragments of flesh and blood against the wall.

My wounds were painful, and the sensation produced was as though a ball had passed through and down the whole length of my leg. I very well remember my reflections at the time. I had a very painful idea of becoming lame and decrepid, and being an object of pity, and I felt as though I would rather die than be placed in such circumstances.

It would seem that immediately after my attempt to leap out of the window, Joseph also did the same thing, of which circumstance I have no knowledge, only from information. The first thing that I noticed was a cry that he had leaped out of the window. A cessation of firing followed, the mob rushed downstairs, and Dr. Richards went to the window. Immediately afterward I saw the doctor going towards the jail door, and as there was an iron door at the head of the stairs, adjoining our door which led into the cells for criminals, it struck me that the doctor was going there, and I said to him, "Stop, Doctor, and take me along." He proceeded to the door and opened it, and then returned and dragged me along to a small cell prepared for criminals.

Brother Richards was very much troubled, and exclaimed, "Oh! Brother Taylor, is it possible that they have killed both Brother Hyrum and Joseph? it cannot surely be, and yet I saw them shoot them;" and elevating his hands two or three times, he exclaimed, "Oh Lord, my God, spare

Thy servants!" He then said, "Brother Taylor, this is a terrible event;" and he dragged me farther into the cell, saying, "I am sorry I can not do better for you;" and, taking an old, filthy mattress, he covered me with it, and said, "That may hide you, and you may yet live to tell the tale, but I expect they will kill me in a few moments." While lying in this position I suffered the most excruciating pain.

Soon afterwards Dr. Richards came to me, informed me that the mob had precipitately fled, and at the same time confirmed my worst fears that Joseph was assuredly dead. I felt a dull, lonely, sickening sensation at the news. When I reflected that our noble chieftain, the Prophet of the living God, had fallen, and that I had seen his brother in the cold embrace of death, it seemed as though there was a void or vacuum in the great field of human existence to me, and a dark gloomy chasm in the kingdom, and that we were left alone. Oh, how lonely was the feeling! How cold, barren and desolate! In the midst of difficulties he was always the first in motion; in critical positions his counsel was always sought. As our Prophet he approached our God, and obtained for us his will; but now our Prophet, our counselor, our general, our leader, was gone, and amid the fiery ordeal that we then had to pass through, we were left alone without his aid, and as our future guide for things spiritual or temporal, and for all things pertaining to this world, or the next, he had spoken for the last time on earth.

These reflections and a thousand others flashed upon my mind. I thought, why must the good perish, and the virtuous be destroyed? Why must God's nobility, the salt of the earth, the most exalted of the human family, and the most perfect types of all excellence, fall victims to the cruel, fiendish hate of incarnate devils?

The poignancy of my grief, I presume, however, was somewhat allayed by the extreme suffering that I endured from my wounds.

Chapter 11

THE DEVIL AND THE CORONER

Soon afterwards I was taken to the head of the stairs and laid there, where I had a full view of our beloved and now murdered brother, Hyrum. There he lay as I had left him; he had not moved a limb; he lay placid and calm, a monument of greatness even in death; but his noble spirit had left its tenement, and was gone to dwell in regions more congenial to its exalted nature. Poor Hyrum! He was a great and good man, and my soul was cemented to his. If ever there was an exemplary, honest, and virtuous man, an embodiment of all that is noble in the human form, Hyrum Smith was its representative.

While I lay there a number of persons came around, among whom was a physician. The doctor, on seeing a ball lodged in my left hand, took a penknife from his pocket and made an incision in it for the purpose of extracting the ball therefrom, and having obtained a pair of carpenter's compasses, made use of them to draw or pry out the ball, alternately using the penknife and compasses. After sawing for some time with a dull penknife, and prying and pulling with the compasses, he ultimately succeeded in extracting the ball, which weighed about half an ounce. Some time afterwards he remarked to a friend of mine, that I had "nerves like the devil" to stand what I did in its extraction. I really thought I had need of nerves to stand such surgical butchery, and that, whatever my nerves may be, his practice was devilish.

This company wished to remove me to Mr. Hamilton's Hotel, the place where we had stayed previous to our incarceration in jail. I told them, however, that I did not wish to go: I did not consider it safe. They protested that it was, and that I was safe with them; that it was a perfect outrage for men to be used as we had been; that they were my friends; that it was for my good they were counseling me, and that I could be better taken care of there than here.

I replied, "I don't know you. Whom am I among? I am surrounded by assassins and murderers; witness your deeds! Don't talk to me of kindness or comfort; look at your murdered victims. Look at me! I want none of your counsel nor comfort. There may be some safety here; I can be assured of none anywhere," etc.

They G___ d_____ their souls to hell, made the most solemn asseverations, and swore by God and the devil, and everything else that they could think of, that they would stand by me to death and protect me. In half an hour every one of them had fled from the town.[1]

Soon after a coroner's jury were assembled in the room over the body of Hyrum. Among the jurors was Captain Smith of the "Carthage Greys," who had assisted in the murder, and the same justice before whom we had been tried. I learned of Francis Higbee as being in the neighborhood. On hearing his name mentioned, I immediately rose and said: "Captain Smith, you are a justice of the peace; I have heard his name mentioned; I want to swear my life against him." I was informed that word was immediately sent to him to leave the place, which he did.

Brother Richards was busy during this time attending to the coroner's inquest, and to the removal of the bodies, and making arrangements for their removal from Carthage to Nauvoo.

When he had a little leisure, he again came to me, and at his suggestion I was removed to Hamilton's Tavern. I felt that he was the only friend, the only person, that I could rely upon in that town. It was with difficulty that sufficient persons could be found to carry me to the tavern; for immediately after the murder a great fear fell upon all the people, and men, women, and children fled with great precipitation, leaving nothing nor anybody in the town but two or three women and children and one or two sick persons.

It was with great difficulty that Brother Richards prevailed upon Mr. Hamilton, hotelkeeper, and his family, to stay; they would not until Brother Richards had given a solemn promise that he would see them protected, and hence I was looked upon as a hostage. Under these circumstances, notwithstanding, I believe they were hostile to the "Mormons", and were glad that the murder had taken place, although they did not actually participate in it; and, feeling that I should be a protection to them they stayed.

The whole community knew that a dreadful outrage had been perpetrated by those villains, and fearing lest the citizens of Nauvoo, as they possessed the power, might have a disposition to visit them with a terrible vengeance, they fled in the wildest confusion. And, indeed, it was with very great difficulty that the citizens of Nauvoo could be restrained. A horrid, barbarous murder had been committed, the most solemn pledge violated, and that, too, while the victims were, contrary to the requirements of the law, putting themselves into the hands of the governor to pacify a popular excitement. This outrage was enhanced by the reflection that our people were able to protect ourselves against not only all the mob, but against three times their number and that of the governor's troops put together. They were also exasperated by the speech of the governor in town.

The whole events were so faithless, so dastardly, so mean, cowardly, and contemptible, without one extenuating circumstance, that it would not have been surprising if the citizens of Nauvoo had arisen, *en masse,* and blotted the wretches out of existence. The citizens of Carthage knew they would have done so under such circumstances, and, judging us by themselves, they were all panic-stricken, and fled. Colonel Markam, too, after his expulsion from Carthage, had gone home, related the circumstances of his ejectment, and was using his influence to get a company to go out. Fearing that when the people heard that their Prophet and Patriarch had been murdered under the above circumstances they might act rashly, and knowing that, if they once got roused, like a mighty avalanche, they would lay the country waste before them and take a terrible vengeance—as none of the Twelve were in Nauvoo, and no one, perhaps, with sufficient influence to control the people,

Dr. Richards, after consulting me, wrote the following note, fearing that my family might be seriously affected by the news. I told him to insert that I was slightly wounded.

Willard Richards' note from Carthage Jail to Nauvoo.

Carthage Jail, 8 o'clock 5 min. P.M. June 27th, 1944.

Joseph and Hyrum are dead. Taylor wounded, not very badly. I am well. Our guard was forced, as we believe, by a band of Missourians from 100 to 200. The job was done in an instant, and the party fled towards Nauvoo instantly. This is as I believe it. The citizens here are afraid of the "Mormons" attacking them; I promise them, no!

[Signed] W. RICHARDS.

N.B.—The citizens promise us protection; alarm guns have been fired.

[Signed] JOHN TAYLOR.[2,3]

I remember signing my name as quickly as possible, lest the tremor of my hand should be noticed, and the fears of my family excited.

A messenger was dispatched immediately with the note, but he was intercepted by the governor, who, on hearing a cannon fired at Carthage, which was to be the signal for the murder, immediately fled with his company, and fearing that the citizens of Nauvoo, when apprised of the horrible outrage, would immediately rise and pursue, he turned back the messenger, who was George D. Grant. A second one was sent, who was treated similarly; and not until a third attempt could news be got to Nauvoo.

Samuel H. Smith, brother to Joseph and Hyrum, was

the first brother I saw after the outrage; I am not sure whether he took the news or not; he lived at the time at Plymouth, Hancock county, and was on his way to Carthage to see his brothers, when he was met by some of the troops, or rather mob, that had been dismissed by the governor, and who were on their way home. On learning that he was Joseph Smith's brother they sought to kill him, but he escaped, and fled into the woods, where he was chased for a length of time by them; but, after severe fatigue, and much danger and excitement, he succeeded in escaping, and came to Carthage. He was on horseback when he arrived, and was not only very much tired with the fatigue and excitement of the chase, but was also very much distressed in feelings on account of the death of his brothers. These things produced a fever, which laid the foundation for his death, which took place the 30th of July. Thus another of the brothers fell a victim, although not directly, but indirectly to this infernal mob.

I lay from about five o'clock until two next morning without having my wounds dressed, as there was scarcely any help of any kind in Carthage, and Brother Richards was busy with the dead bodies, preparing them for removal. My wife Leonora started early the next day, having had some little trouble in getting a company or a physician to come with her; after considerable difficulty she succeeded in getting an escort, and Dr. Samuel Bennett came along with her. Soon after my father and mother arrived from Oquakie, near which place they had a farm at that time, and hearing of the trouble, hastened along.

General Deming, brigadier-general of the Hancock

THE DEVIL AND THE CORONER

county militia, was very much of a gentleman, and showed me every courtesy, and Colonel Jones also was very solicitous about my welfare.

I was called upon by several gentlemen of Quincy and other places, among whom was Judge Ralston, as well as by our own people, and a medical man extracted a ball from my left thigh that was giving me much pain; it lay about half an inch deep, and my thigh was considerably swollen. The doctor asked me if I would be tied during the operation; I told him no; that I could endure the cutting associated with the operation as well without, and I did so; indeed, so great was the pain I endured that the cutting was rather a relief than otherwise.

A very laughable incident occurred at the time; my wife, Leonora, went into an adjoining room to pray for me, that I might be sustained during the operation. While on her knees at prayer, a Mrs. Bedell, an old lady of the Methodist association, entered, and, patting Mrs. Taylor on her back with her hand, said: "There's a good lady, pray for God to forgive your sins; pray that you may be converted, and the Lord may have mercy on your soul."

The scene was so ludicrous that Mrs. Taylor knew not whether to laugh or be angry. Mrs. Taylor informed me that Mr. Hamilton, the father of the Hamilton who kept the house, rejoiced at the murder, and said in company that it was done up in the best possible style, and showed good generalship, and she farther believed that the other branches of the family sanctioned it. These were the associates of the old lady referred to, and yet she could talk of conversion and saving souls in the midst of blood and murder: such is man and such consistency!

The ball being extracted was the one that first struck me, which I before referred to; it entered on the outside of my left thigh, about five inches from my knee, and passing rather obliquely towards my body, had, it would seem, struck the bone, for it was flattened out nearly as thin and large as a quarter of a dollar.

NOTES

1. The doctor who dislodged the bullet from John Taylor's left hand with the carpenter's compass and dull penknife was Thomas L. Barnes, of Carthage. In November of 1897, he wrote a letter to his daughter Miranda Barnes Haskett briefly describing the massacre at Carthage. In addition to other details, the letter recounts John Taylor's condition when found in the cell by the jailer (Mr. Steghall). Though not completely accurate (e.g., Dr. Barnes fails to mention the bullet that lodged in John Taylor's left knee), it presents a singular account of Elder Taylor's emergence from the cell, his condition, and the extent of his wounds, other than his own account. The original spelling is preserved [MT]:

> . . . I suppose by this time you are anxious to know what became of Taylor and Richards; was they also killed, no they were not. Taylor was severely wounded Richards was not hurt. Shall I try to describe the wounds that Taylor received and got over them. Well let me tell you where we found him, I cannot impress your mind of his appearance as he appered to us when we wer called to him by the jailer. We found him in a pile of straw. It appeared that a straw bed had been emtied in the cell where he was when we found him. He was very much frightened as well as severly wounded. It took strong persuading of the jailer as well as our positive assuriance that we ment him no harm but was desirous of doing him some good. He finally consented to come out of his cell. When we examined him we found that he had been hit by four balls. One ball had hit him in his for arm and pased down and lodged in the hand between the

phalanges of his third and fourth fingers [the one dislodged by Dr. Barnes—MT]. Another hit on the left side of the pelvis cuttin through the skin and pasing _____ leaving a superficial wound that you could lay your hand in. A third ball passed through his thigh lodging in his notus. A fourth ball hit his watch which had in the fob in his pantaloons, which I suppose the Mormons have today, to show the precise time that their great leader was killed. The wounds had bled quite freely, the blood had had time to coagulate which it had done, and where the clothes and straw came in contact they all adhered together so that Mr. Taylor came out of his self sought cell he was a pitable looking sight. We took the best care of him we could till he left us. He got well but never paid us for skill or good wishes.

2. *Deseret News,* no. 38, 25 November 1857, p. 297 [JT].

3. Elder Richards wrote more than one note to be sent to Nauvoo. As indicated by the one included in the Martyrdom Manuscript, he wrote the first at about 8:00 P.M. on the evening of the day of the Martyrdom. In addition, he wrote a second note (and made at least one, but perhaps more than one) copy of it. At the time of this printing (1999), the archives of the Church retain two originals. These also contain John Taylor's "shaky" signature. Ironically, Elder Taylor further instructed Elder Richards to play down the severity of his wounds, as indicated in the text of the second note. Also note that Governor Ford and General Demming, who had returned to Carthage, appended comments onto the bottom of the note [MT]:

12 o'clock at night, 27ᵗʰ June
Carthage, Hamilton's Tavern

To Mrs. Emma Smith and Major-General Dunham, &c.:

The Governor has just arrived; says all things shall be inquired into, and all right measures taken. I say to all the citizens of Nauvoo, my brethren, be still, and that *God reigns. Don't rush out of the city*—don't rush to Carthage—stay at home, and be prepared for an attack from Missouri robbers. The Governor will render every assistance possible—has sent out orders for troops. Joseph and Hyrum are dead. We will prepare to move the bodies as soon as possible. The people of the county are greatly excited, and fear the Mormons will come out and take vengeance. I have pledged my word the Mormons will stay at home as soon as they can be informed, and no violence will be on their part, and say to my brethren in Nauvoo, in the name of the Lord, be still, be patient, only let such friends as choose come here and see the bodies. Mr. Taylor's wounds are dressed and not serious. I am sound.

(Signed) WILLARD RICHARDS
JOHN TAYLOR

Defend yourselves until protection can be furnished necessary, June 27th 1844

(Signed) THOMAS FORD,
Governor and Commander-in-Chief

Mr. Orson Spencer:

Dear Sir:—Please deliberate on this matter—prudence may obviate material destruction. I was at my residence when this horrible crime was committed. It will be condemnned by three-fourths of the citizens of the country. Be quire, or you will be attacked from Missouri.

(Signed) M. R. DEMMING

Chapter 12

ANALYZING GOVERNOR FORD'S COMPLICITY

The governor passed on, staying at Carthage only a few minutes, and he did not stop until he got fifty miles from Nauvoo.

There had been various opinions about the complicity of the governor in the murder, some supposing that he knew all about it, and assisted or winked at its execution. It is somewhat difficult to form a correct opinion; from the facts presented it is very certain that things looked more than suspicious against him.

In the first place, he positively knew that we had broken no law.

Secondly. He knew that the mob had not only passed inflammatory resolutions, threatening extermination to the "Mormons", but that they had actually assembled armed mobs and commenced hostilities against us.

Thirdly. He took those very mobs that had been arrayed against us, and enrolled them as his troops, thus legalizing their acts.

Fourthly. He disbanded the Nauvoo Legion, which had never violated law, and disarmed them, and had about his person in the shape of militia known mobocrats and violators of the law.

Fifthly. He requested us to come to Carthage without arms, promising protection, and then refused to interfere in delivering us from prison, although Joseph and Hyrum were put there contrary to law.

Sixthly. Although he refused to interfere in our behalf, yet, when Captain Smith went to him and informed him that the persons refused to come out, he told him that he had a command and knew what to do, thus sanctioning the use of force in the violation of law when opposed to us, whereas he would not for us interpose his executive authority to free us from being incarcerated contrary to law, although he was fully informed of all the facts of the case, as we kept him posted in the affairs all the time.

Seventhly. He left the prisoners in Carthage jail contrary to his plighted faith.

Eighthly. Before he went he dismissed all the troops that could be relied upon, as well as many of the mob, and left us in charge of the "Carthage Greys," a company that he knew were mobocratic, our most bitter enemies, and who had passed resolutions to exterminate us, and who had been placed under guard by General Deming only the day before.

Ninthly. He was informed of the intended murder, both before he left and while on the road, by several different parties.

Tenthly. When the cannon was fired in Carthage, signifying that the deed was done, he immediately took up his line of march and fled. How did he know that this signal portended their death if he was not in the secret? It may be said some of the party told him. How could he believe what the party said about the gun signal if he could not believe the testimony of several individuals who told him in positive terms about the contemplated murder?

He has, I believe, stated that he left the "Carthage Greys" there because he considered that, as their town was contiguous to ours, and as the responsibility of our safety rested solely upon them, they would not dare suffer any indignity to befall us. This very admission shows that he did really expect danger; and then he knew that these people had published to the world that they would exterminate us, and his leaving us in their hands and taking of their responsibilities was like leaving a lamb in charge of a wolf, and trusting to its humanity and honor for its safe- keeping.

It is said, again, that he would not have gone to Nauvoo, and thus placed himself in the hands of the "Mormons", if he had anticipated any such event, as he would be exposed to their wrath. To this it may be answered that the "Mormons" did not know their signals, which he did; and they were also known in Warsaw, as well as in other places; and as soon as the gun was fired, a merchant of Warsaw jumped upon his horse and rode directly to Quincy, and reported, "Joseph and Hyrum killed, and those who were with them in jail." He reported farther that "they were attempting to break jail, and were all killed by the guard." This was their story; it was anticipated to kill all, and the gun was to be the signal that the deed was accomplished. This was known in Warsaw. The governor also knew it and fled; and he could really be in no danger in Nauvoo, for the Mormons did not know it, and he had plenty of time to escape, which he did.

It is said that he made all his officers promise solemnly that they would help him to protect the Smiths; this may or may not be. At any rate, some of these same officers helped to murder them.

The strongest argument in the governor's favor and one that would bear more weight with us than all the rest put together, would be that he could not believe them capable of such atrocity and thinking that their talk and threatenings were a mere ebullition of feeling, a kind of braggadocio, and that there was enough of good moral feeling to control the more violent passions, he trusted to their faith. There is, indeed, a degree of plausibility about this, but when we put it in juxtaposition to the amount of evidence that he was in possession of it weighs very little. He had nothing to inspire confidence in them, and everything to make him mistrust them. Besides, why his broken faith? Why his disregard of what was told him by several parties? Again, if he knew not the plan how did he understand the signal? Why so oblivious to everything pertaining to the "Mormon" interest, and so alive and interested about the mobocrats? At any rate, be this as it may, he stands responsible for their blood, and it is dripping on his garments. If it had not been for his promises of protection, they would have protected themselves; it was plighted faith that led them to the slaughter; and to make the best of it, it was a breach of that faith and a non-fulfillment of that promise, after repeated warnings, that led to their death.

Having said so much, I must leave the governor with my readers and with his God. Justice, I conceive, demanded this much, and truth could not be told with less; as I have said before, my opinion is that the governor would not have planned this murder, but he had not sufficient energy to resist popular opinion, even if that opinion led to blood and death.

It was rumored that a strong political party, numbering in its ranks many of the prominent men of the nation, were engaged in a plot for the overthrow of Joseph Smith, and that the governor was of this party, and Sharp, Williams, Captain Smith and others were his accomplices, but whether this was the case or not I do not know. It is very certain that a strong political feeling existed against Joseph Smith, and I have reason to believe that his letters to Henry Clay were made use of by political parties opposed to Mr. Clay, and were the means of that statesman's defeat. Yet, if such a combination as the one referred to existed, I am not apprised of it.

THE HOMECOMING

―

While I lay at Carthage, previous to Mrs. Taylor's arrival, a pretty good sort of man, who was lame of a leg, waited upon me, and sat up at night with me; after Mrs. Taylor, my mother and others waited upon me.

Many friends called upon me, among whom were Richard Ballantyne, Elizabeth Taylor, several of the Perkins family, and a number of the brethren from Macedonia and La Harpe. Besides these, many strangers from Quincy, some of whom expressed indignant feelings against the mob and sympathy for myself. Brother Alexander Williams called upon me, who suspected that they had some designs in keeping me there, and stated that he had at a given point in some woods, fifty men, and if I would say the word he would raise other fifty, and fetch me out of there. I thanked him, but told him I thought there was no need. However, it would seem that I was in some danger; for Colonel Jones, before referred to, when absent from me, left two loaded pistols on the table in case of an attack, and some time afterwards, when I had recovered and was publishing the affair, a lawyer, Mr. Backman, stated that he had prevented a man by the name of Jackson, before referred to, from ascending the stairs, who was coming with a design to murder me, and that now he was sorry he had not let him do the deed.

There were others also, of whom I heard, that said I ought to be killed, and they would do it, but that it was too damned cowardly to shoot a wounded man; and thus, by the chivalry of murderers, I was prevented from being a second time mutilated or killed. Many of the mob came around and treated me with apparent respect, and the officers and people generally looked upon me as a hostage, and feared that my removal would be the signal for the rising of the "Mormons".

I do not remember the time that I stayed at Carthage, but I think three or four days after the murder, when Brother Marks with a carriage, Brother James Allred with a wagon, Dr. Ells, and a number of others on horseback, came for the purpose of taking me to Nauvoo. I was very weak at the time, occasioned by the loss of blood and the great discharge of my wounds, so when my wife asked me if I could talk I could barely whisper no. Quite a discussion arose as to the propriety of my removal, the physicians and people of Carthage protesting it would be my death, while my friends were anxious for my removal if possible.

I suppose the former were actuated by the above-named desire to keep me. Colonel Jones was, I believe, sincere; he had acted as a friend all the time, and he told Mrs. Taylor she ought to persuade me not to go, for he did not believe I had strength enough to reach Nauvoo. It was finally agreed, however, that I should go; but as it was thought that I could not stand riding in a wagon or carriage, they prepared a litter for me; I was carried downstairs and put upon it. A number of men assisted to carry me, some of whom had been engaged in the mob. As soon as I got downstairs, I felt much better and strengthened, so that I could talk; I suppose the effect of the fresh air.

When I had got near the outside of the town, I remembered some woods that we had to go through, and telling a person near to call for Dr. Ells, who was riding a very good horse, I said: "Doctor, I perceive that the people are getting fatigued with carrying me; a number of 'Mormons' live about two or three miles from here, near our route; will you ride to their settlement as quick as possible, and have them come and meet us!" He started off on a gallop immediately. My object in this was to obtain protection in case of an attack, rather than to obtain help to carry me.

Very soon after the men from Carthage made one excuse after another, until they had all left, and I felt glad to get rid of them. I found that the tramping of those carrying me produced violent pain, and a sleigh was produced and attached to the hind end of Brother James Allred's wagon, a bed placed upon it, and I propped up on the bed. Mrs. Taylor rode with me, applying ice water to my wounds. As the sleigh was dragged over the grass on the prairie, which was quite tall, it moved very easily and gave me very little pain.

When I got within five or six miles of Nauvoo the brethren commenced to meet me from the city, and they increased in number as we grew nearer, until there was a very large company of people of all ages and both sexes, principally, however, men.

For some time there had been almost incessant rain, so that in many low places on the prairie it was from one to three feet deep in water, and at such places the brethren whom we met took hold of the sleigh, lifted it, and carried it over the water, and when we arrived in the neighborhood of the city, where the roads were excessively muddy and bad, the brethren tore down the fences, and we passed through the fields.

Never shall I forget the differences of feeling that I experienced between the place that I had left and the one that I had now arrived at. I had left a lot of reckless, blood-thirsty murderers, and had come to the City of the Saints, the people of the Living God; friends of truth and righteousness, thousands of whom stood there with warm, true hearts to offer their friendship and services, and to welcome my return. It is true it was a painful scene, and brought sorrowful remembrance to my mind, but to me it caused a thrill of joy to find myself once more in the bosom of my friends, and to meet with the cordial welcome of true, honest hearts. What was very remarkable, I found myself very much better after my arrival at Nauvoo than I was when I started my journey, although I had traveled eighteen miles.

Chapter 14

THE MIRACLE

———

The next day, as some change was wanting, I told Mrs. Taylor that if she could send to Dr. Richards, he had my purse and watch, and they would find money in my purse.

Previous to the doctor leaving Carthage, I told him that he had better take my purse and watch, for I was afraid the people would steal them. The doctor had taken my pantaloon's pocket, and put the watch in it with the purse, cut off the pocket, and tied a string around the top; it was in this position when brought home. My family, however, were not a little startled to find that my watch had been struck with a ball. I sent for my vest, and, upon examination it was found that there was a cut as if with a knife, in the vest pocket which had contained my watch. In the pocket the fragments of the glass were found literally ground to powder. It then occurred to me that a ball had struck me at the time I felt myself falling out of the window, and that it was this force that threw me inside. I had often remarked to Mrs. Taylor the singular fact of finding myself inside the room, when I felt a moment before, after being shot, that I was falling out, and I never could account for it until then; but here the thing was fully elucidated, and was rendered plain to my mind. I was indeed falling out, when some villain aimed at my heart. The ball struck my watch, and forced me back; if I had fallen out I should assuredly have been killed, if not by the fall, by those around, and this ball, intended to dispatch me, was turned by an overruling Providence into a messenger of mercy, and saved my life. I shall never forget the feelings of gratitude that I then experienced towards my heavenly Father; the whole scene was vividly portrayed before me, and my heart melted before the Lord. I felt that the Lord had preserved me by a special act of mercy; that my time had not yet come, and that I had still a work to perform upon the earth.[1]

(Signed) JOHN TAYLOR

NOTE

1. At the time of this printing (1999) John Taylor's watch (visibly damaged on its face) was on permanent display in the Church Historical Museum west of Temple Square in Salt Lake City [MT].

JOHN TAYLOR'S NOTES

In addition to the above I give the following:—

Dr. Bernhisel informed me that Joseph, looking him full in the face, and as solemn as eternity said: "I am going as a lamb to the slaughter, but I am as calm as a summer's morning. I have a conscience void of offense toward God and man." I heard him state, in reply to an interrogatory, made either by myself or some one in my hearing, in relation to the best course to pursue: "I am not now acting according to my judgment; others must counsel, and not me, for the present," or in words to the same effect.

The governor's remarks about the press may be partially correct, so far as the legal technicality was concerned, and the order of administering law. The proper way would perhaps have been for the city council to have passed a law in regard to the removal of nuisances, and then for the municipal court to have ordered it to be abated on complaint. Be this as it may, it was only a variation in form, not in fact, for the municipal court formed part of the council, and all voted; and furthermore, some time after the murder, Governor Ford told me that the press ought to have been removed, but that it was bad policy to remove it as we did; that if we had only let a mob do it, instead of using the law, we could have done it without difficulty, and no one would have been implicated. Thus the governor, who would have winked at the proceedings of a mob, lent his aid to, or winked at, the proceedings of mob violence in the assassination of Joseph and Hyrum Smith for removing a nuisance according to law, because of an alleged informality in the legal proceedings or a legal technicality.

I must here state that I do not believe Governor Ford would have planned the murder of Joseph and Hyrum Smith; but being a man that courted popular opinion, he had not the firmness to withstand the mob, even when that mob were seeking to imbrue their hands in the blood of innocence; he lent himself to their designs and thus became a partaker of their evil deeds.

I will illustrate this vexed question with the following official paper, which appeared in the *Deseret News,* No. 30:—

> Two of the brethren arrived this evening (June 13th, 1844), from Carthage, and said that about 300 mobbers were assembled there, with the avowed intention of coming against Nauvoo. Also that Hamilton [the hotel proprietor] was paying a dollar per bushel for corn to feed their animals.

The following was published in the *Warsaw Signal Office;* I insert it as a specimen of the unparalleled corruption and diabolical falsehood of which the human race has become capable in this generation:—

> At a mass meeting of the citizens of Hancock county,

convened at Carthage on the 11th day of June, 1844, Mr. Knox was appointed President, John Doty and Lewis F. Evans, Vice-presidents, and William Y. Head, Secretary.

Henry Stephens, Esq., presented the following resolutions, passed at a meeting of the citizens of Warsaw, and urged the adoption of them as the sense of this meeting:

PREAMBLE AND RESOLUTIONS

Whereas information has reached us, about which there can be no question, that the authorities of Nauvoo did recently pass an ordinance declaring a printing press and newspaper published by the opponents of the Prophet a nuisance, and in pursuance thereof did direct the marshal of the city and his adherents to enter by force the building from whence the paper was issued, and violently (if necessary) to take possession of the press and printing materials, and thereafter to burn and destroy the same; and whereas, in pursuance of said ordinance, the marshal and his adherents, together with a mob of Mormons, did, after sunset on the evening of the 10th inst., violently enter said building in a tumultuous manner, burn and destroy the press and other materials found on the premises;

And whereas Hyrum Smith did, in the presence of the city council and the citizens of Nauvoo, offer a reward for the destruction of the printing press and materials of the *Warsaw Signal,*—a newspaper also opposed to his interest:

And whereas the liberty of the press is one of the cardinal principles of our government, firmly guaranteed by the several Constitutions of the states, as well as the United States;

And whereas Hyrum Smith has within the last week publicly threatened the life of one of our valued citizens, Thos. C. Sharp, the editor of the *Signal:*

Therefore be it solemnly *Resolved* by the citizens of Warsaw in public meeting assembled,

That we view the recent ordinance of the city of Nauvoo, and the proceedings thereunder, as an outrage of an alarming character, revolutionary and tyrannical in its tendency, and being under color of law, as calculated to subvert and destroy in the minds of the community all reliance on the law.

Resolved, That as a community we feel anxious, when possible, to redress our grievances by legal remedies; but the time has now arrived when the law has ceased to be a protection to our lives and property; a mob at Nauvoo, under a city ordinance, has violated the highest privilege in our government, and to seek redress in the ordinary mode would be utterly ineffectual.

Resolved, That the public threat made in the council of the city not only to destroy our printing press, but to take the life of its editor, is sufficient, in connection with the recent outrage, to command the efforts and the services of every good citizen to put an immediate stop to the career of the mad Prophet and his demoniac coadjutors. We must not only defend ourselves from danger, but we must resolutely carry the war into the enemy's camp. We do therefore declare that we will sustain our press and the editor at all hazards. That we will take full vengeance—terrible vengeance, should the lives of any of our citizens be lost in the effort. That we hold ourselves at all times in readiness to cooperate with our fellow citizens in this state, Missouri, and

Iowa, to *exterminate,* UTTERLY EXTERMINATE, the wicked and abominable Mormon leaders, the authors of our troubles.

Resolved, That a committee of five be appointed forthwith to notify all persons in our township suspected of being the tools of the Prophet to leave immediately on pain of INSTANT VENGEANCE. And we do recommend the inhabitants of the adjacent townships to do the same, hereby pledging ourselves to render all the assistance they may require.

Resolved, That the time, in our opinion, has arrived when the adherents of Smith as a body, all be driven from the surrounding settlements into Nauvoo; that the Prophet and his miscreant adherents should then be demanded at their hands, and if not surrendered, A WAR OF EXTERMINATION SHOULD BE WAGED, to the entire destruction, if necessary for our protection, of his adherents. And we do hereby recommend this resolution to the consideration of the several townships to the mass convention to be held at Carthage, hereby pledging ourselves to aid to the utmost the complete consummation of the object in view, that we may thereby be utterly relieved of the alarm, anxiety, and trouble to which we are now subjected.

Resolved, That every citizen arm himself, to be prepared to sustain the resolutions herein contained.

Mr. Roosevelt rose and made a brief but eloquent speech, and called upon the citizens throughout the country to render efficient aid in carrying out the spirit of the resolutions. Mr. Roosevelt then moved that a committee of seven be appointed by the chair to draft resolutions expressive of our action in future.

Mr. Catlin moved to amend the motion of Mr. Roosevelt so that the committee should consist of one from each precinct; which motion as amended, was adopted.

The chair then appointed the following as said committee:—Col. Levi Williams, Rocky Run precinct; Joel Catlin, Augusta; Samuel Williams, Carthage; Elisha Worrell, Chili; Capt. Maddison, St. Mary's; John M. Ferris, Fountain Green; James Rice, Pilot Grove; John Carns, Bear Creek; C. L. Higbee, Nauvoo; George Robinson, La Harpe; and George Rockwell, Warsaw.

On motion of Mr. Sympson, Walter Bagby, Esq. was requested to address the meeting during the absence of the committee. He spoke long and eloquently upon the cause of our grievances, and expressed his belief that the time was now at hand when we were individually and collectively called upon to repel the innovations upon our liberties, and suggested that points be designated as places of encampment at which to rendezvous our forces, that we may be ready, when called upon, for efficient actions.

Dr. Barns, one of the persons who went with the officers to Nauvoo for the purpose of arresting the rioters, having just arrived, came into the meeting, and reported the results of their proceedings,—which was, that the persons charged in the writs were duly arrested, but taken from the officer's hands on a writ of *habeas corpus* from the municipal court, and discharged, and the following potent words entered upon the records—HONORABLY DISCHARGED.

On motion of O. C. Skinner, Esq., a vote of thanks

was tendered to Dr. Barns for volunteering his services in executing said writs.

Francis M. Higbee was now loudly called for. He stated his personal knowledge of the Mormons from their earliest history, throughout their hellish career in Missouri and this state, which had been characterized by the darkest and most diabolical deeds which had ever disgraced humanity.

The committee appointed to draft resolutions brought in the following report, which after some considerable discussion, was unanimously adopted:

REPORT OF THE COMMITTEE

Whereas the officer charged with the execution of a writ against Joseph Smith and others, for riot in the county of Hancock, which said writ said officer has served upon said Smith and others; and whereas said Smith and others refuse to obey the mandate of said writ; and whereas, in the opinion of this meeting, it is impossible for the said officer to raise a *posse* of sufficient strength to execute said writ; and whereas, it is the opinion of this meeting, that the riot is still progressing, and that violence is meditated and determined on, it is the opinion of this meeting that the circumstances of the case require the interposition of executive power: Therefore,

Resolved, That a deputation of two discreet men be sent to Springfield, to solicit such interposition.

2nd. *Resolved,* That a said deputation be furnished with a certified copy of the resolution, and be authorized to obtain evidence by affidavit and otherwise in regard to the violence which has already been committed, and is still farther meditated.

Dr. Evans here rose and expressed his wish that the above resolutions would not retard our operations, but that we would each one arm and equip ourselves forthwith.

The resolutions passed at Warsaw were again read by Dr. Barns, and passed by acclamation.

On motion of A. Sympson, Esq., the suggestion of Mr. Bagby, appointing places of encampment, was adopted to wit: Warsaw, Carthage, Green Plains, Spilman's Landing, Chili, and La Harpe.

On motion, O. C. Skinner and Walter Bagby, Esqrs. were appointed a committee to bear the resolutions adopted by this meeting to his excellency the governor, requiring his executive interposition.

On motion of J. H. Sherman, a Central Corresponding Committee was appointed.

Ordered, That J. H. Sherman, H. T. Wilson, Chauncey Robinson, Wm. S. Freeman, Thomas Morrison, F. M. Higbee, Lyman Prentiss, and Stephen H. Tyler be said committee.

On motion of George Rockwell,

Resolved, That constables in the different precincts hold themselves in readiness to obey the officer in possession of the writs, whenever called upon, in summoning the *posse.*

On motion, the meeting adjourned.

> JOHN KNOX, President.
> JOHN DOTY,
> LEWIS F. EVANS,
>   Vice Presidents.

W. Y. HEAD, Secretary.

The following will conclude the "*Expositor* Question":
Nauvoo, June 14th, 1844.

JOSEPH SMITH'S ACCOUNT
OF THE *EXPOSITOR* AFFAIR

SIR,—I write you this morning briefly to inform you of the facts relative to the removal of the press and fixtures of the *Nauvoo Expositor* as a nuisance.

The 8th and 10th instant were spent by the city council of Nauvoo in receiving testimony concerning the character of the *Expositor,* and the character and designs of the proprietors.

In the investigation it appeared evident to the council that the proprietors were a set of unprincipled, lawless debauches, counterfeiters, bogus-makers, gamblers, peace-disturbers, and that the grand object of said proprietors was to destroy our constitutional rights and chartered privileges; to overthrow all good and wholesome regulations in society; to strengthen themselves against the municipality; to fortify themselves against the church of which I am a member, and destroy all our religious rights and privileges by libels, slanders, falsehoods, perjury, etc., and sticking at no corruption to accomplish their hellish purposes, and that said paper of itself was libelous of the deepest dye, and very injurious as a vehicle of defamation, tending to corrupt the morals, and disturb the peace, tranquility, and happiness of the whole community, and especially that of Nauvoo.

After a long and patient investigation of the character of the *Expositor,* and the characters and designs of its proprietors, the Constitution, the Charters (see addenda to Nauvoo Charter from the *Springfield Charter,* sec. 7), and all the best authorities on the subject (see *Blackstone* iii. 5, and n. etc. etc.), the city council decided that is was necessary for the "peace, benefit, good order, and regulations" of said city, "and for the protection of the property," and for "the happiness and prosperity of the citizens of Nauvoo," that said *Expositor* should be removed; and declaring said *Expositor* a nuisance, ordered the Mayor to cause them to be removed without delay, which order was committed to the Marshal by due process, and by him executed the same day, by removing the paper, press, and fixtures into the streets, and burning the same; all which was done without riot, noise, tumult, or confusion, as has already been proved before the municipality of the city; and the particulars of the whole transaction may be expected in our next *Nauvoo Neighbour.*

I send you this hasty sketch that your excellency may be aware of the lying reports that are now being circulated by our enemies, that there has been a *"mob at Nauvoo,"* and *"blood and thunder,"* and *"swearing that two men were killed,"* etc. etc., as we hear from abroad, are false—false as satan himself could invent, and that nothing has been transacted here but what has been in perfect accordance with the strictest principles of law and good order on the part of the authorities of this city; and if your excellency is not satisfied, and shall not be satisfied, after reading the whole proceedings, which will be forthcoming soon, and shall demand an investigation of our municipality before Judge Pope, or any legal tribunal at the Capitol, you have only to write your wishes and we will be forthcoming; we will not trouble you to file a writ or send an officer for us.

I remain as ever, a friend of truth, good order,
And your excellency's humble servant,
[Signed] JOSEPH SMITH

His Excellency Thomas Ford.

Part *3*

—

EPILOGUE AND
APPENDICES

———

After the Martyrdom Elder Taylor recuperated at his home. The severity of his wounds required him to remain essentially idle for several weeks; his life hung in the balance for some time.

The entire Carthage experience had, by any measure, become a tremendously defining moment for him. Six years previously, he had been summoned to Far West, Missouri, having received word from Joseph Smith that he had been appointed to fill a vacancy in the Council of the Twelve. At the council meeting where his ordination occurred, he testified before the Council of the Twelve that he was willing to do whatever the Lord might require at his hand. Little did he know then what would soon come upon him in consequence of his loyalty to his newfound faith and to the Prophet Joseph Smith.

He had, as a new convert of less than two years, established his loyalty publicly in defending the Prophet Joseph Smith before an excited crowd in the Kirtland Temple. In that meeting in the temple, one of Joseph's most outspoken critics, Warren Parrish, had delivered a violent attack upon Joseph's character. Toward the close of the meeting, John Taylor stood to address the assembly, and boldly defended the Prophet and his calling and warned that the combative spirit manifested in that meeting would lead to rebellion and idolatry as it had done with the children of Israel when they began to criticize Moses' prophetic calling.

But testifying before a crowd was one thing, and defending the Prophet before a mob of assassins was quite another. In Carthage John Taylor took to the prophet's defense again, as he stood before the assassins and, with a hickory stick, attempted to deflect the shower of balls coming from the mob's muskets in peril of his own life. He demonstrated his willingness to sacrifice all he had, even his own life if necessary, for the kingdom of God on the earth. There can be no question that the Carthage experience, and the suffering that occurred afterward, defined and refined who John Taylor was and where his allegiance lay, the theme of which would surface again and again throughout the remainder of his life. He would be called upon repeatedly to stand up in the Church's defense throughout the more than forty years that would remain in his apostolic career.

While the remaining members of the Council of the Twelve were returning to Nauvoo after the martyrdom, Elders Taylor and Richards stood as presiding officers. They immediately wrote an article in the *Times and Seasons,* on 1 July 1844, addressed to the branches of the Church, urging the Saints to remain steadfast in the faith and to be peaceable citizens. They stated that as soon as the Twelve, or a majority of them, could assemble, the future course of the Church would be decided.

As the other members of the Twelve returned to Nauvoo and the need for councils arose, they met in Elder Taylor's home to transact the business of the Church until Elder Taylor had sufficiently convalesced from his wounds.

Under the direction of Quorum President Brigham Young, they dealt with the aftermath of the martyrdom and pushed forward with the construction of the Nauvoo Temple.

For a time, Joseph's demise seemed to calm the opposition, but the reprieve was short-lived. It was not long before the Twelve were forced by their persecutors to begin addressing the enormous task of organizing and pushing forward the plans for the westward migration of the Saints to the Rocky Mountains.

Ultimately Elder Taylor's wounds healed, but he retained a slight limp in his stride, which became more noticeable as he aged. That limp was most likely the result of the bullet that had lodged in his left knee at Carthage and which was never removed—the bullet he let his children feel and instructed them never to forget how it got there. Any disability he retained, however, failed to slow the pace of his ministry. His miraculous preservation further confirmed, unmistakably in his mind, that the Lord did indeed have a work for him yet to accomplish, and seldom did any other pursuit distract his efforts.

Elder Taylor is probably best known for the years he served as president of The Church of Jesus Christ of Latter-day Saints. Yet that service was only the culminating commitment to the kingdom which began in 1836 in Toronto, Canada, where he had accepted the message of the restoration.

Elder Taylor's conversion to the gospel is interwoven with a marvelous prophecy that Elder Heber C. Kimball delivered to Parley P. Pratt in Kirtland, Ohio, in 1836. In that year Elder Pratt was in debt, his wife was in ill health, and the couple was still childless after many years of marriage. One evening after Elder and Sister Pratt had retired, Elder Kimball awakened them and delivered the following message:

> Brother Parley, thy wife shall be healed from this hour, and shall bear a son. . . . Arise, therefore, and go forth in thy ministry, nothing doubting. . . . Thou shalt go to Upper Canada, even to the city of Toronto . . . and there thou shalt find a people prepared for the gospel, and they shall receive thee, and thou shalt organize the Church among them . . . and from things growing out of this mission, shall the fulness of the gospel spread into England, and cause a great work to be done in that land.[1]

At the time, John Taylor, though affiliated with the Methodist church, had become dissatisfied with the wide differences between modern and primitive Christianity. He had organized a study group with several other brethren for the purpose of investigating the doctrines of Christianity as contained in the Bible. Through their studies, the group concluded that all sects were in error and without authority to preach the gospel or administer its ordinances. The group eventually attracted the attention of the local Methodist authorities who convened a hearing. The ministers decided to censure the group's doctrines, strip them of any ecclesiastical offices, but retain them as members. The motion carried, but members of the study group continued to fast and pray that if God had a people on the earth who possessed the authority to preach and administer the ordinances of the gospel, that he would send one of their ministers to them.

In the meantime, shortly after Elder Kimball's visit, Elder Pratt ventured to Toronto. Upon his arrival, a local merchant who was acquainted with John Taylor and his study group gave Elder Pratt a letter of introduction and directions to the Taylors' home. John Taylor's initial reaction to Elder Pratt was anything but congenial, he having heard some of the "shades" of Mormonism previously. It wasn't long, however, before his initial biases toward the traveling Mormon subsided and he began to discover some grounds for entertaining Pratt's message.[2]

Elder Pratt was eventually introduced to the meetings held by John Taylor and his group of Methodist dissenters, and they were most intrigued with the Apostle's message. Soon afterward, John declared that he would make an earnest investigation of Mormonism and began following Elder Pratt from place to place, recording his sermons and comparing them with scripture. Conviction soon came, and John and his wife Leonora were baptized 8 May 1836. They immersed themselves in the new life of the restored gospel.

Elder Taylor quickly began his labors in the ministry, being ordained an elder in the Church soon after his baptism. He was set apart to preside over the branches in Canada in August of that year. In March of the following year, Elder Taylor visited Kirtland, Ohio, and there met the Prophet Joseph Smith, who entertained him at his home and tutored him on several points of doctrine. He returned to Canada with renewed strength in his efforts in the ministry. When the Prophet Joseph Smith, accompanied by

Sidney Rigdon and Thomas B. Marsh, visited Canada in August 1837, Elder Taylor assisted him in organizing conferences throughout the area, whereupon Joseph ordained Elder Taylor a high priest before returning to Kirtland. It was in the fall of 1837 that Heber C. Kimball's prophecy to Elder Parley P. Pratt regarding the spreading of the gospel from Canada to England came to fruition—in part through the efforts of John Taylor. At the request of Elder Joseph Fielding, John Taylor wrote to Elder Fielding's brother, a minister in Preston, England, regarding the restoration of the gospel. That letter became the first announcement of the Restoration in that land. Upon announcement of Elder Taylor's call to the apostleship, the Prophet also requested that Elder Taylor remove to Far West, which he and his family did, arriving in Far West in the fall of 1838. Between that time and the time of the Martyrdom, Elder Taylor was ordained to the apostleship. He also experienced the persecutions in Missouri, removed his family to Illinois, and fulfilled a mission to England with the other members of the Twelve. Upon his return to Nauvoo, he founded the *Nauvoo Neighbor,* a local newspaper, and became the editor of *The Times and Seasons,* all the while establishing himself as a writer and publisher and "watchman on the tower."

Among the more significant tasks that Elder Taylor confronted in the period after the martyrdom was the westward migration. He and his family departed Nauvoo on 16 February 1846 with eight wagons, a carriage, and the necessary teams. Along with the other members of the Church, he found that getting across Iowa proved to be an ominous venture. Resources were meager, and traveling conditions were terrible. The journey became extremely tedious as the spring rains relentlessly fell on the migrating companies, turning the entire route into a formidable mud bog. But the Taylors eventually arrived in Council Bluffs, Iowa, on the Missouri River, in June 1846, about four months after departing Nauvoo.

Soon after the leading companies had arrived at Council Bluffs, the Twelve received word that some of the brethren who had been set apart as Church leaders in Great Britain were committing certain acts of apostasy and iniquity. Elders John Taylor, Parley P. Pratt, and Orson Pratt were appointed to return to England to reestablish order and cleanse the Church. They departed for England in early July 1846, leaving behind their families and trusting that the Lord would protect and care for their loved ones until their return.

The brethren performed the duties to which they had been assigned. Afterward, Elder Taylor visited other branches of the Church in England, Scotland, and Wales. He returned to the States and was able to reunite with his family at Council Bluffs on 25 March 1847, just a few days prior to the departure of Brigham Young's company of trail-breaking pioneers.

Upon his return to Council Bluffs, Elder Taylor learned that he and Elder Pratt had been appointed to lead the first large company of settlers to the Rocky Mountains, following behind the pioneer company. The huge Pratt–Taylor wagon train departed Winter Quarters on 21 June 1847,[3] following the trail blazed by President Young's company of pioneers. The trek was long and arduous, but Elder Taylor's company reached the valley of the Great Salt Lake on 5 October 1847.

During the thirty plus years that Brigham Young presided over the Church, Elder Taylor was called upon by the President to fulfill numerous assignments relating to his role as an Apostle. Because Elder Taylor possessed an unusual command of the English language, President Young placed him in circumstances where those talents could be best put to use.

Shortly after Elder Taylor settled his family in Salt Lake City, Brigham Young called him to serve a series of missions at home and abroad. In 1849, President Young sent him to open missions in both France and Germany. While in Europe, he arranged for and supervised the translation of the Book of Mormon into French and German. On that mission, he had numerous opportunities to defend the faith and its founder, and he returned to the Valley in 1852. In the spring of 1853, he was set apart to preach the gospel of Jesus Christ in the "valleys of the mountains." In fulfilling that mission he visited nearly every settlement and outlying community in Utah, delivering the message with which he had been charged to the members of the Church.

In the meantime, the Church had gone public with a principle of its faith, the doctrine of celestial marriage, which included the plurality of wives. No sooner did the announcement come, than misrepresentation distorted the doctrine into everything vile and impure. Utah quickly became looked upon as a hotbed of impurity. In responding to the resulting tide of misunderstanding, President

Young sent several of the Twelve to establish newspapers across the nation. He gave Elder Taylor the assignment of establishing a paper in the heartland of journalism—New York City. Taking up the challenge squarely, Elder Taylor established the paper right between the city's two newspaper giants. To one side of *The Mormon's* headquarters were the offices of the New York *Herald,* and to the other were the offices of the *Tribune.*

However, the available resources to begin a paper were meager. Elder Taylor had to raise funds to get the paper off the ground, as the Church could not provide the required means.[4] Yet, he somehow managed, and the first edition of *The Mormon* hit the streets of New York on 1 February 1855. In launching the paper, he charged into the battle in his early editorials and defied "all the editors and writers in the United States" to legitimately prove that "Mormonism was less moral, scriptural, philosophical."[5] His defense of his faith was fearless and reminiscent of the role he had played in Carthage. His articles were cogent and elegant, bearing the king's English in forceful style and attesting to Elder Taylor's unbending loyalty to the Church and its president.

In conjunction with his publishing mission, he had also been assigned to preside over the Eastern States Mission of the Church. Those efforts occupied his time until the fall of 1857, at which time he was called home.

In the 1860s and 1870s, the current of anti-Mormon sentiments became more intense from both political and other sources, including preachers of other churches. Elder Taylor took every opportunity to defend the rights of the

Saints through the medium of the public press, at home and abroad.

One incident in which his talents and influence reached beyond Church circles to a broad public audience occurred when Elder Taylor engaged the vice president of the United States, Schyler Colfax, in a debate in the press in 1869. Colfax came to Utah several times to attempt to persuade the Church's leaders to concede to public opinion regarding the practice of plural marriage. Then, in a public address on his second visit, the vice president derided the Saints for placing God's laws higher than the laws of the land, stabbing sharply at President Young's authority as the Lord's mouthpiece. Elder Taylor, who was on a proselytizing mission to Boston at the time, promptly responded to the vice president's comments in a reply that was published in the New York *Tribune* and in the *Deseret News* in Salt Lake City. He attacked the vice president's address, suggesting that eastern society (i.e., the federal government) should clean up its own act and that the vice president should attend to the ills of society, such as crime, divorce, infanticide, and prostitution, before attempting to save the Mormons. When Elder Taylor returned to Salt Lake City, he became known as the "lion of the valley." Never before had the position of the Church been so masterfully presented and defended. And when his stinging reply induced Colfax to prepare a retort, Elder Taylor responded with a series of five letters to the New York *Herald* that were reproduced by the *Deseret News* and distributed worldwide. These letters formed an eloquent statement of the current circumstances, persuasively outlining the Church's side of the conflict with the federal government, as well as the abuses heaped upon the Church by local federal officials—"petty lords of misrule"—in Salt Lake City. The letters stated the Saints' position in a way the many readers in the nation could understand, if not appreciate and empathize with. Many years later, Elder B. H. Roberts wrote that "taking it all in all, [the public exchange between Elder Taylor and the vice president] is doubtless the most important in the history of the Church."[6]

In addition to making significant literary contributions in Church periodicals and the public press, Elder Taylor also made important contributions in doctrine and doctrinal clarification. In 1852 while on his mission to France and Germany, he wrote *The Government of God,* which continues as a doctrinal reference work today. *Items on Priesthood,* which he wrote in 1877, provided new instruction to bishops and other priesthood leaders regarding the origins, transactions, and powers of the priesthood. Elder Taylor also placed renewed emphasis to the Savior's mission and its center place in Mormon doctrine in his book *The Mediation and Atonement of Our Lord and Savior Jesus Christ,* written in 1880.

In June 1875, new responsibilities were placed upon Elder Taylor when President Young clarified Elder Taylor's position in the Quorum of the Twelve. There had been confusion for some time over the issue of seniority in the Twelve. Of those called to the original Quorum of the Twelve under Joseph Smith, only Brigham Young, Orson Hyde, and Orson Pratt remained. But in 1839, Orson Hyde had resigned his position in the Twelve in the face of differences with Joseph Smith. Elder Hyde later returned to the Twelve and assumed his former position. Further, Orson Pratt apostatized briefly from 1842 to 1843. He too assumed his former position with the Twelve on his return. Even Wilford Woodruff, who was ordained to the Twelve after Elder Taylor, had been inadvertently placed on the records of the time as senior to Elder Taylor, perhaps because Elder Woodruff was slightly older than Elder Taylor. Having been ordained on 19 December 1838, Elder Taylor had stood in the circle and assisted in ordaining Elder Woodruff to the Twelve when the quorum met on the cornerstone of the temple foundation at Far West, Missouri, on 26 April 1839.

As a counselor in the First Presidency, Elder George A. Smith initiated discussion among the First Presidency about the matter, whereupon President Young was moved to act and did so at a council meeting in Sanpete County, Utah, in 1875. President Young asserted that seniority was based on length of time in the quorum and on no other basis. Elders Hyde and Pratt lost their seniority when they departed from the Twelve, and Elders Taylor and Woodruff automatically assumed their places. Hence, Elder Taylor was the senior Apostle, Elder Woodruff next, followed by Elders Hyde and Pratt, respectively. In proclaiming the change to the council, President Young turned toward Elder Taylor and declared, "Here is the man whose right it is to preside over the council in my absence, he being the senior Apostle."[7]

Elder Taylor had known of the discrepancies in the seniority of the Twelve long before President Young made the change, but had remained silent on the matter, choosing not to "agitate or bring up a question of that kind."[8] This realignment, which had been brought about through no action on Elder Taylor's part, was ratified by the Twelve and then by the members of the Church in the October general conference. The new role that Elder Taylor assumed as president of the Council of the Twelve brought new challenges and blessings to his life, as he directed the activities of the Twelve throughout the world.

Despite the high offices to which they had been called, President Young and Elder Taylor were no strangers to friendly banterings. The President had great respect for Elder Taylor's literary and missionary talents and had, on several occasions, made that respect publicly known. However, the President might have been a little envious of Elder Taylor's social refinement and his proper gentlemanly English style. President Young was in discussion one day with several members of a particular family in his office, having left the door to the office ajar. As a group of people walked by, President Young noticed the tall, handsome, and immaculately dressed person of Elder John Taylor. Perhaps feeling somewhat outdone in fashion, President Young declared, "Well, if there isn't Prince John!" Hearing the comment as he passed by, and being quite capable of defending himself, Elder Taylor returned to the office door and retorted, "As a person, Brigham Young, you can be awfully small; but I still respect you as a great leader."[9]

It wasn't long after he was sustained as president of the Council of the Twelve Apostles that Elder Taylor's responsibilities were measurably increased again. Brigham Young, who had presided over the Church for more than three decades after the martyrdom and under whose direction the Church had grown and flourished in the desert wilderness, experienced a significant decline in health in the summer of 1877. He passed away 25 August of that year. Shortly thereafter, Elder Taylor, as senior Apostle, was sustained as the Church's leader and eventually as President of The Church of Jesus Christ of Latter-day Saints.

At the time of President Young's death, the political, economic, and social challenges the Church faced were severe. But Elder Taylor seemed to have been prepared to face these difficult times. Understanding that the body of the Church could weather the challenges more effectively if the members were of one mind, he set about to strengthen and unify the Church from within. To that end, the year 1880, the fiftieth anniversary of the Church's organization, was proclaimed the Year of the Jubilee in the tradition of the Old Testament. Under President Taylor's direction, the Church sponsored remarkable, large-scale celebrations and forgave a large portion of the debts that immigrating Latter-day Saints had incurred. Further, President Taylor also authorized new editions of the scriptures to be published that year.

President Taylor also continued to expand the base of settlements that President Young had established, authorizing the founding of more than one hundred additional communities. He pushed forward construction on the Salt Lake and Manti temples and saw the completion of the Logan Temple, dedicating it in a series of sessions that began 17 May 1884. He also continued to use his literary talents to defend the Church and its doctrines.

Organizationally, President Taylor restructured the Church's auxiliary programs. Having been involved in the women's organization from the day of its inauguration, he commissioned Eliza R. Snow to visit the settlements of the Church in the West to revitalize the Relief Society, the Young Women's Mutual Improvement Association, and the children's Primary association. He appointed members of the Council of the Twelve to direct the affairs of the Sunday School and Young Men's Mutual Improvement Association.

Many of Elder Taylor's sermons and writings tended to reveal a fierceness or boldness in his temperament, especially when he was defending or upholding a principle of the gospel. But he also had a tender side that was, perhaps, magnified as a result of his brush with death in Carthage. That tenderness was revealed on one occasion in which conditions could have easily justified not responding to the needs at hand. When he and his family crossed the Mississippi River into Iowa after their departure from Nauvoo in 1846, one of his children—perhaps young Joseph—became inconsolable for several days. Finally, the parents were able to assess that the child missed a treasured rocking horse, which they had required be left behind with many other belongings in the Taylor mansion in Nauvoo. Fully aware of the danger in which he would place himself if he returned to Nauvoo, Elder Taylor disguised himself, crossed the river under the cover of night, and retrieved the horse, which provided comfort on the journey.[10]

That sensitive side of Elder Taylor's nature is also revealed in many of his administrative interactions with the members of the Church. He seemed to have an enduring patience for their struggles, always seeking to build them up and encourage them onward. An example of this disposition involved the calling of a new stake president. A young, successful businessman, not yet twenty-five, was considered for the position of stake president of one of the Church's stakes in western Utah. The man was interviewed by President Taylor and his counselor Joseph F. Smith, and the man reluctantly accepted the position. The man's name was announced in the morning session of the conference. He was invited to stand and say a few remarks, and he did so. After the session concluded, Presidents Taylor and Smith retreated to the home of the former stake president for lunch. During that time, President Smith remarked to the new stake president that he hadn't borne testimony that he knew the Church was true in his remarks. "Don't you know with every fiber of your soul that this church is the only true church on the earth?" President Smith asked.

"No, I don't," came the reply. "I believe it is the only true church, but I don't know it."

Dumbfounded by what he had heard, President Smith turned to President Taylor and said, "President Taylor, I move that we return to this afternoon's session and undo everything that we did this morning. I don't think we should allow a man to be the president of a stake unless he knows the Church is true."

The man responded, "Well, President Smith, I don't. I did not seek this position, and I would only be too happy to be relieved of it."

Speechless at this revelation, President Smith gaped at President Taylor in disbelief. But President Taylor gave a hearty laugh, and throwing back his head, he retorted, "Joseph, Joseph, Joseph! This man knows that the Church is true just as much as you and I. The only thing that he does not know is that he does know it. And it will be but a short time before he is able to bear testimony that the Church is true. We will not undo what we have done this morning."

Indeed, the man was sustained in his position, and it wasn't long before that knowledge did come, and fervent testimony was borne. The rest of the story is that fewer than two years later, the man was called to fill a vacant position in the Council of the Twelve. That man was none other than Heber J. Grant, who years later was sustained to the same position President Taylor had then held as president of the Church.[11]

Sadly, during the period of time when the visibility of key Church leaders was especially needed in the crisis over plural marriage, President Taylor (joining several other key Church leaders) reluctantly withdrew from the public eye for the protection of his own family, the Church, and himself. Having recently returned home from a tour of Church units in the Southwest, he preached his last public sermon on 1 February 1885 in the Tabernacle on Temple Square, and moved his life to the underground, thereafter. Little did those in attendance at that meeting know that they would never see him again.

Although he still conducted Church business while in the underground, that life quickly took its toll on his physical condition. His body was taxed by the physical and mental strain of having to be continually on the move, evading federal marshals who were attempting to enforce what he considered to be flagrantly unconstitutional anti-polygamy laws. Although he was able to spend much of his time in familial circles, he longed to be among his own family members. Yet, he seldom complained, and he continued to show sensitivity to those who cared for him.

On one stopover in Parowan, Utah, during the holiday season of 1885, he stayed with Bishop Charles Adams and family. He freed himself from the stresses of underground life by taking part in caring for the children of the home. In the evenings he would put them in his lap, tell them stories, and sing to them. On Christmas morning as the children were unwrapping their gifts, he was elated to find that Sister Adams had knitted him a pair of socks from wool that she had washed, carded, and spun. "See! I have the best present of all!" he teased. Removing his shoes and socks, he exclaimed, "A pair of nice warm stockings to keep my tootsie wootsies warm!" Gaping at his long, bony, bunion-ridden feet, the children giggled and blushed. Giggling all the more they retorted that "tootsie wootsies" were baby feet. Chuckling in reply, he rejoined, "Well, I'm being babied here, aren't I?"[12]

Eventually President Taylor's physical condition fell prey to the pressures of confinement. His health began failing in the summer of 1887. Joseph F. Smith, then in the Sandwich Islands, was immediately notified to return home, as the president's health was in imminent danger. Days before President Taylor's passing, President Smith arrived, and the three men of the presidency, President John Taylor, President George Q. Cannon, and President Joseph F.

Smith, were together for the first time in three and a half years. Though he was very weak when President Smith arrived, President Taylor exclaimed, "I feel to thank the Lord!" He passed away quietly on 25 July 1887 in Kaysville, Utah.

John Taylor viewed his mission in life with simplicity. As president of the Church, he reiterated that view, the seeds which had been sown in his heart by the Spirit of the Lord long before he had even heard the word *Mormon.* He stated:

> My mission was to preach the gospel of salvation to the nations of the earth, and I have traveled hundreds of thousands of miles to do this, without purse or scrip, trusting in the Lord.[13]

In significant ways, the conclusion of John Taylor's life paralleled that of his esteemed Prophet as a martyr for the truth; like the Prophet, President Taylor died for his beliefs.

President Taylor suffered the tremendous pains of a gradual loss of health in the confinement of the underground. His counselors, in announcing his passing, memorialized him as a double martyr, as they read a tribute that had been penned in his behalf many years before. Shortly after the martyrdom, on 27 July 1844, Sister Eliza R. Snow, well known for her skillful poetic abilities, and sensing the magnitude and depth of the experience through which Elder Taylor had passed in Carthage, penned the following lines in his honor. Her verses appeared in the 1 August 1844 edition of the *Times and Seasons* (with textual and grammatical usage preserved):

TO ELDER JOHN TAYLOR

Thou Chieftain of Zion! henceforward thy name
Will be class'd with the martyrs and share in their fame,
Thro' ages eternal, of thee will be said,
'WITH THE GREATEST OF PROPHETS HE SUFFER'D AND BLED.

When the shafts of injustice were pointed at HIM—
When the cup of his suff'ring was fill'd to the brim—
When his innocent blood was inhumanly shed,
You shar'd his afflictions and with him you BLED.

When around you like hailstones the rifle balls flew—
When the passage of death opened wide to your view—
When the prophet's freed spirit, thro' martyrdom fled,
In your gore you lay welt'ring—with the martyrs you BLED.

All the SCARS from your WOUNDS, like the trophies of yore
Shall be ensigns of honor till you are no more;
And by all generations, of thee shall be said,
'WITH THE BEST OF THE PROPHETS, IN PRISON HE BLED.

Indeed, John Taylor was and is remembered as a survivor of the carnage of Carthage. And that experience defined much of who and what he became. His life attests to his fearlessness and courage in standing up for what he believed and knew to be right. Like the lives of his two predecessors in the Presidency, his life was in some ways a type and shadow of the Savior's. Though each walked a unique path, like all of the Lord's anointed in both the former and latter-day work, their lives are testimonies of the Savior and of the Restoration He has brought to pass in this dispensation. John Taylor died with a price on his head, but faithful to the errand on which the Lord had sent him. He viewed the source of the confinement under which he had been restricted in the latter years of his life as persecution and a flagrant violation of his constitutional rights. Had circumstances been otherwise, he may have lived another decade. But it was not to be. President John Taylor had fulfilled the work for which he had been preserved so many years ago in an obscure village jail in Illinois.

NOTES

1. *Autobiography of Parley P. Pratt* (Salt Lake City: Deseret Book, 1976), pp. 130–31.

2. In reality, John's wife Leonora saved the day. John had dismissed Elder Pratt on their first encounter without listening to his message. When Pratt returned the next afternoon to say good-bye to the Taylors, as he had not had any success in finding a place to preach in the city, a neighbor of the Taylors, Mrs. Walton, unexpectedly stopped by. Leonora told Mrs. Walton about Elder Pratt's plight, concluding, "He may be a man of God, I am sorry to have him depart." Mrs. Walton immediately invited Elder Pratt to her home to make use of a "spare room and bed and food in plenty," as well as "two large rooms to preach in." Probably on the encouragement of his wife Leonora, and not being able to resist hearing what the missionary had to say, the Taylors attended the meeting at Mrs. Walton's that evening, where Elder Pratt gave his first sermon. Shortly thereafter John Taylor declared his intention to investigate the message. See B. H. Roberts, *The Life of John Taylor* (Salt Lake City: George Q. Cannon and Sons, 1892), p. 36.

3. Compared to the advance pioneer company of 148 people, the Pratt–Taylor company was a behemoth, consisting of 600 wagons, 1,553 souls, 2,213 oxen, 124 horses, 887 cows, 358 sheep, 716 chickens and a few pigs.

4. Elder Taylor commented to President Young in a letter, "How long we shall be able to continue [to publish *The Mormon*], I don't know. We are doing as well as we can, and shall continue to do so; but I find it one thing to preach the gospel without purse or scrip, and another thing to publish a paper on the same terms."

5. *The Mormon,* vol. 1, no. 1.

6. B. H. Roberts, *The Life of John Taylor* (Salt Lake City: G. Q. Cannon and Sons, 1892), p. 309.

7. George Q. Cannon in *Journal of Discourses* (London: John Henry Smith, 1883), 23:365.

8. G. Homer Durham, *The Gospel Kingdom* (Salt Lake City: Bookcraft, 1943), p. 192.

9. This story was told by William R. Wallace, noted pioneer irrigation engineer, who as a young boy was a personal witness to the event. See Leonard J. Arrington, *Brigham Young: American Moses* (New York: Alfred A. Knopf, 1985), p. 198.

10. That rocking horse is, at the time of this writing, displayed in the Taylor mansion in Nauvoo, Illinois.

11. Francis M. Gibbons, *Heber J. Grant: Man of Steel, Prophet of God* (Salt Lake City: Deseret Book Co., 1979), pp. 39–41, 44–48.

12. As told by Eleanor Ward Ogden, niece to Bishop Charles Adams. See Samuel Taylor, *The Kingdom or Nothing: The Life of John Taylor, Militant Mormon* (New York: Macmillan, 1976), p. 352.

13. *Journal of Discourses*, 22:142–43.

Immediately following the Martyrdom, the Twelve determined to formally announce the deaths of Joseph and Hyrum Smith. That task fell upon Elder John Taylor. The text of that announcement provides a great legacy. In announcing the martyrdom, Elder Taylor described some events omitted from the Martyrdom Manuscript and memorialized Joseph and his contributions to the latter days in an expressive manner not found elsewhere. Accordingly, I include the text in its entirety below. Elder Taylor's efforts were ultimately added to the canon of Church scripture as Doctrine and Covenants Section 135:

DOCTRINE & COVENANTS SECTION 135

To seal the testimony of this book and the Book of Mormon, we announce the martyrdom of Joseph Smith the Prophet, and Hyrum Smith the Patriarch. They were shot in Carthage jail, on the 27th of June, 1844, about five o'clock p.m., by an armed mob—painted black—of from 150 to 200 persons. Hyrum was shot first and fell calmly, exclaiming: *I am a dead man!* Joseph leaped from the window, and was shot dead in the attempt, exclaiming: *O Lord my God!* They were both shot after they were dead, in a brutal manner, and both received four balls.

2 John Taylor and Willard Richards, two of the

Twelve, were the only persons in the room at the time; the former was wounded in a savage manner with four balls, but has since recovered; the latter, through the providence of God, escaped, without even a hole in his robe.

3 Joseph Smith, the Prophet and Seer of the Lord, has done more, save Jesus only, for the salvation of men in this world, than any other man that ever lived in it. In the short space of twenty years, he has brought forth the Book of Mormon, which he translated by the gift and power of God, and has been the means of publishing it on two continents; has sent the fulness of the everlasting gospel, which it contained, to the four quarters of the earth; has brought forth the revelations and commandments which compose this book of Doctrine and Covenants, and many other wise documents and instructions for the benefit of the children of men; gathered many thousands of the Latter-day Saints, founded a great city, and left a fame and name that cannot be slain. He lived great, and he died great in the eyes of God and his people; and like most of the Lord's anointed in ancient times, has sealed his mission and his works with his own blood; and so has his brother Hyrum. In life they were not divided, and in death they were not separated!

4 When Joseph went to Carthage to deliver himself up to the pretended requirements of the law, two or three days previous to his assassination, he said: "I am going like a lamb to the slaughter; but I am calm as a summer's morning; I have a conscience void of offense towards God, and towards all men. I SHALL DIE INNOCENT, AND IT SHALL YET BE SAID OF ME—HE WAS

MURDERED IN COLD BLOOD."—The same morning, after Hyrum had made ready to go—shall it be said to the slaughter? yes, for so it was—he read the following paragraph, near the close of the twelfth chapter of Ether, in the Book of Mormon, and turned down the leaf upon it:

5 *And it came to pass that I prayed unto the Lord that he would give unto the Gentiles grace, that they might have charity. And it came to pass that the Lord said unto me: If they have not charity it mattereth not unto thee, thou hast been faithful; wherefore thy garments shall be made clean. And because thou hast seen thy weakness, thou shalt be made strong, even unto the sitting down in the place which I have prepared in the mansions of my Father. And now I . . . bid farewell unto the Gentiles; yea, and also unto my brethren whom I love, until we shall meet before the judgment-seat of Christ, where all men shall know that my garments are not spotted with your blood.* The testators are now dead, and their testament is in force.

6 Hyrum Smith was forty-four years old in February, 1844, and Joseph Smith was thirty-eight in December, 1843; and henceforward their names will be classed among the martyrs of religion; and the reader in every nation will be reminded that the Book of Mormon, and this book of Doctrine and Covenants of the church, cost the best blood of the nineteenth century to bring them forth for the salvation of a ruined world; and that if the fire can scathe a green tree for the glory of God, how easy it will burn up the dry trees to purify the vineyard of corruption. They lived for glory; they died for glory; and glory is their eternal reward.

From age to age shall their names go down to posterity as gems for the sanctified.

7 They were innocent of any crime, as they had often been proved before, and were only confined in jail by the conspiracy of traitors and wicked men; and their *innocent blood* on the floor of Carthage jail is a broad seal affixed to "Mormonism" that cannot be rejected by any court on earth, and their *innocent blood* on the escutcheon of the State of Illinois, with the broken faith of the State as pledged by the governor, is a witness to the truth of the everlasting gospel that all the world cannot impeach; and their *innocent blood* on the banner of liberty, and on the *magna charta* of the United States, is an ambassador for the religion of Jesus Christ, that will touch the hearts of honest men among all nations; and their *innocent blood,* with the innocent blood of all the martyrs under the altar that John saw, will cry unto the Lord of Hosts till he avenges that blood on the earth. Amen.

H aving had extensive personal contact with the Prophet
Joseph Smith, Elder John Taylor wrote a great deal
about him. He frequently defended the Prophet in his
public discourses. The following summarizes how he felt
about the Prophet. He made the statement in Boulougne-
Sur-Mer, France, in 1855 on his mission to France. The
statement in defense of the Prophet was made during three
nights of public debate with three ministers of other
churches. The three had made slanderous comments about
the Prophet, whereupon Elder Taylor said the following in
his defense:

> I testify that I was acquainted with Joseph Smith
> for years. I have traveled with him; I have been with
> him in private and in public; I have associated with him
> in councils of all kinds; I have listened hundreds of
> times to his public teachings, and his advice to his
> friends and associates of a more private nature. I have
> been at his house and seen his deportment in his family.
> I have seen him arraigned before the tribunals of his
> country, and have seen him honorably acquitted, and
> delivered from the pernicious breath of slander, and
> the machinations and falsehoods of wicked and corrupt
> men. I was with him living, and with him when he died,
> when he was murdered in Carthage jail by a ruthless
> mob . . . with their faces painted. I was there and was

myself wounded; I at that time received four balls in my body. I have seen him, then, under these various circumstances, and I testify before God, angels, and men, that he was a good, honorable, virtuous man—that his doctrines were good, scriptural, and wholesome—that his precepts were such as became a man of God—that his private and public character was unimpeachable—and that he lived and died as a man of God and a gentleman. This is my testimony.[1]

Elder Taylor had deep feelings about the gospel of Jesus Christ and its applications in mortal life. Those feelings, which he developed during the process of his conversion, provided the foundation for his courage to defend the Prophet Joseph Smith against mobs and to preach the gospel to the nations of the earth. They were the foundation of all that he believed and did. The following forcefully summarizes his views on the breadth of the gospel's application to mortality. He wrote this on July 28, 1855, as part of an editorial in *The Mormon,* the New York City newspaper he was publishing and managing at the time:

The everlasting gospel . . . is adapted to the wants of the human family, to the world morally, socially, religiously and politically. It is not a sickly, sentimental, effeminate plaything; not a ghostly, spiritual, sing-song, ethereal dream, but a living, sober, matter-of-fact reality, adapted to body and spirit, to earth and heaven, to time and eternity. It enters into all the ramifications of life. It does not adapt itself to the philosophy, politics, creeds, and opinions of men, but fashions them in its divine mold. It cannot be twisted into the multitudinous latitudinarian principles of a degenerate world;

but lifts all that are in the world, who will be subject to its precepts, to its own ennobling, exalted and dignified standard. It searches all truth, and grasps at all intelligence; it is the revealed living and abiding will of God to man; a connection between the heavens and the earth; it is nature, philosophy, heavens and earth, time and eternity united. It is the philosophy of the heavens and the earth, of God, and angels, and saints.[2]

NOTES

1. *The Gospel Kingdom,* sel. G. Homer Durham (Salt Lake City: Deseret Book Co., 1943), p. 355.
2. Ibid., pp. 2–3.

Index

INDEX

INDEX

Morrison, Thomas, 37–38, 68, 81, 123

Nauvoo: abandonment of, 5; threats to, 23; Legion, 24–25, 40; martial law declared at, 41; council convened in, 51; guarding of, 73; reaction to martyrdom, 98; John Taylor returns to, 112; Saints to be driven from, 120

Nauvoo Expositor, 30, 68, 74; Joseph Smith's account of the incident with, 124–26

Nauvoo Legion, 24–25, 40, 68–69; Governor Ford disbands, 106

Nauvoo Neighbor, 4, 29, 34, 125, 134

Nauvoo Temple, 131

Nauvoo Times and Seasons, 4, 29, 34, 130, 134; tribute to John Taylor in, 148

Newspapers: interference with, 29, 34–35; establishment of, 137

New York Herald, 137–39

New York Mormon, 7, 137, 156–57

Norton, Henry O., 63

Notes, source of, 17

Ogle County, 27

Ordinances, 131

Parrish, Warren, 129

Perry, Stephen, 37–38

Persecution, of Latter-day Saints, 23–24, 131

Phelps, William W.: writ issued against, 37–38; returns to Nauvoo, 57

Pistol, 83, 89

Politicians, 25, 109

Pope, Judge, 125

Pratt-Taylor wagon train, 135–36

Pratt, Orson, 135, 139–40

Pratt, Parley P., 131–32, 134; mission of, 133; returns to England, 135

Prentiss, Lyman, 123

Press: liberty of the, 32–34, 118; Gov. Ford on, 68, 116–17; Joseph Smith on, 70, 124–26; Taylor uses to defend Saints, 137–38; destruction of, 161

Priesthood, 139

Primary, 143

Prophet: Joseph Smith's mission as, 6

Protection, governor pledges, 51

Quorum of the Twelve, 139–40

Ralston, Judge, 101

Redfield, Harvey D., 37–38

Reed, Mr., 61, 79

Relief Society, 143

Religionists, 25

Restoration, the, 3

Rice, James, 121

Richards, Levi, 37–38

Richards, Willard, 82; secretary to Joseph Smith, 4; death of, 6; and *Nauvoo Expositor,* 33; leaves Nauvoo, 53–54; returns to Nauvoo, 57; at Carthage, 88–93, 97, 151–52; sends note from Carthage Jail, 99; and John Taylor's watch, 114; and Council of the Twelve, 130

Rigdon, Sidney, 134

Rights, equal, 70

Roberts, B. H., and Martyrdom Manuscript, 15–16

Robinson, Chauncey, 123

Robinson, George, 121

I N D E X

Rockwell, George, 121, 123
Rockwell, Porter: writ issued
 against, 37
Rocky Mountains, 3, 131, 135

Saints: extermination of, 24, 26,
 34–35, 120; mobs threaten
 extermination of, 40–41, 59, 75,
 105; westward migration of, 131,
 134–35
Salt Lake Temple, 142
Salt Lake Valley, 12, 14
Scoundrels, 26–27
Scriptures, new editions of, 142
Settlements, Church, 142
Sharp, Thomas C., 28, 109, 119
Sherman, J. H., 123
Skinner, O. C., 80–81, 121–23
Smith, George A., 140
Smith, Robert F., 60–61, 80, 83; at
 inquest, 96; and Governor Ford,
 106, 109
Smith, Elias, 54, 57
Smith, George A., 7–9; reports to
 Brigham Young, 10; and John
 Taylor, 21
Smith, Hyrum: death of, 3; writ
 issued against, 37–38; and letter
 from governor, 52; leaves
 Nauvoo, 53–54; returns to
 Nauvoo, 57; leaves for Carthage,
 59–60; accused of treason, 63;
 incarcerated at Carthage, 66;
 asks John Taylor to sing, 84;
 martyrdom of, 88–93; character
 of, 95; imprisonment of, 106;
 assassination of, 117; and
 destruction of *Warsaw Signal,*
 118; announcement of death of,
 151–54
Smith, John, 82

Smith, Joseph, Jr.: death of, 3, 5;
 persecutors of, 3–5; and *Nauvoo
 Expositor,* 30–32; writ issued
 against, 37–38; forwards
 affidavits to Ford, 39–40, 49;
 informed of Ford's arrival, 43;
 summoned to Carthage, 50–51;
 and letter from governor, 43–44;
 leaves Nauvoo, 53–54; returns to
 Nauvoo, 57; leaves for Carthage,
 59–60; accused of treason, 63;
 incarcerated at Carthage, 66;
 interview with governor, 67; on
 the Constitution, 70; on
 imprisonment at Carthage, 72;
 mob conspires against, 79;
 receives pistol from Cyrus
 Wheelock, 83; martyrdom of,
 89–93; imprisonment of, 106;
 political party conspires against,
 109; on martyrdom, 116;
 assassination of, 117; writ for
 arrest of, 122; account of
 Nauvoo Expositor affair by,
 124–26; meets John Taylor, 133;
 announcement of death of,
 151–54; and the Book of
 Mormon, 152; contact of, with
 John Taylor, 155–56
Smith, Joseph F., 144, 146–47
Smith, Robert F., 64
Smith, Samuel H., 99–100
Snow, Eliza R., 143, 147–48
Speech, liberty of, 32–34, 68
Spencer, Augustine, 63
Statehood, Utah, 7
Steghall George W., 81–82
Stephens, Henry, 118
Sunday School, 143
Sympson, A., 121, 123

Taylor, Elizabeth, 110